Wall Art

Wall Art

35 FRESH AND STRIKING PROJECTS TO DECORATE YOUR WALLS

CLARE YOUNGS

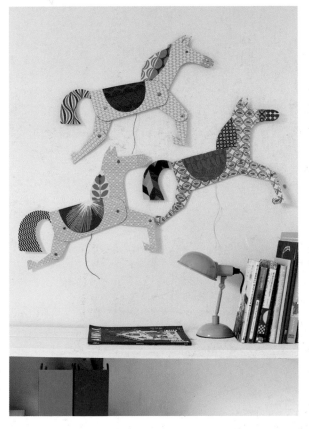

CICO BOOKS
LONDON NEW YORK

Published in 2015 by CICO Books
An imprint of Ryland Peters & Small Ltd
20–21 Jockey's Fields   341 E 116th St
London   New York, NY
WC1R 4BW   10029

www.rylandpeters.com

10 9 8 7 6 5 4 3 2 1

A CIP catalog record for this book is
available from the Library of Congress
and the British Library.

ISBN: 978-1-78249-247-4

Printed in China

Editor: Anna Southgate
Designer: Elizabeth Healey
Photographer: Joanna Henderson
Illustrator: Ian Youngs
Stylist: Clare Youngs

In-house editor: Anna Galkina
In-house designer: Fahema Khanam
Art director: Sally Powell
Production controller: David Hearn
Publishing manager: Penny Craig
Publisher: Cindy Richards

Contents

Introduction

When planning how to furnish your apartment, house, or student room, art is unlikely to be the first thing you think about. First, you need somewhere comfortable to sit and sleep, a storage system, and a floor covering. No matter how thrifty and smart you are, these things cost money. Your budget may be blown and the last thing to consider will be what to put on the walls. Like an empty page in my sketchbook, a plain white wall cries out to be filled. A good choice of art can bring an entire room together—providing a focal point, drawing you in, and adding a splash of color. We can't all commission an artist or visit art galleries to buy the paintings of our dreams, but with a bit of help from the projects in this

book, you will be able to fill your space with exciting, fun, and beautiful creations.

Art does not have to be on a canvas. Fill a series of box frames with postcards, scraps of giftwrap, and vintage ephemera and arrange them in a group on the wall. Or collect found objects, such as feathers, dried leaves, pebbles, and shells for an ever-changing display of nature in the home. Paint directly onto a wall for a big statement piece that grabs attention and shouts look at me!

If you have a smart phone, a piece of glass from a picture frame, and a posterboard (cardboard) box, then you can put together a projector in minutes, that will transform a small drawing into a massive image. A projector, a pencil, and a roll of washi tape is all you need to make a giant, geometric hare, leaping across the wall or a stunning Pop Art face in neon pink. Remember that, for these pieces, the cost is minimal. You are not investing in an expensive work of art to last a lifetime.

Traditional crafts, such as macramé and weaving, are big news in the world of interiors at the moment. These projects take a little longer to complete, but the crafts are wonderful to learn and, once you have mastered the techniques, you will be able to create beautiful and unique pieces to add character and a bit of boho chic to your space.

I have used paper, wood, fabric, living plants, paint, rope, and even sticky dots to create 35 very different projects. They are designed to be adapted. We live in a world of mass production where you can put together a look—be it contemporary, rustic, vintage, or industrial—from chain stores. But we also want to express our individuality and add our own personality in the space we make our home. This book is all about that. Use these ideas, learn the techniques, and have the confidence to develop your own unique designs. Be bold. Be brave. Unleash the artist in you and go create some amazing walls!

Techniques

Enlarging templates

Some of the templates on pages 138–143 will need to be enlarged. Each template is clearly marked at the percentage of actual size that it is printed, so you will need to enlarge it to the size it is to be used at. For example, if a template is marked as being 25% of actual size, this means that it is a quarter of its actual size and will need to be increased by 400% (four times its size). To do this, enlarge by 200% on a photocopier, and then enlarge that photocopy by another 200%. If a template is 50% of actual size, then it is half of its actual size and will need to be enlarged by 200%. Some projects will need to be bigger than ledger size (A3). For these, the templates will have to be enlarged in sections and then joined together with tape.

You will need

Large posterboard (cardboard) box and lid measuring approx. 15 x 11 in. (38 x 28 cm), with a depth of 13½ in. (34 cm)

Ruler

Pencil

Craft knife

Small posterboard (cardboard) box and lid measuring approx. 3½ x 3½ in. (9 x 9 cm), with a depth of 5½ in. (14 cm)

Sheet of glass

Masking tape

Black felt-tip pen

Smart phone or torch

Making and using a projector

1 On one side of the large box, cut out a panel measuring 9 in. high by 7 in. wide (22 x 18 cm), using a craft knife.

2 Cover all edges of the sheet of glass with masking tape, to ensure there are no sharp edges.

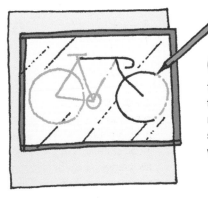

3 When you are ready to project, draw the design onto the glass using a black felt-tip pen. Place the glass over the hole in the large cardboard box and secure with masking tape. (The image will be reversed, so make sure you tape the glass the correct way for your design.)

4 Turn on the torch on your smart phone and tape it to the small box. If you don't have a smart phone, find the brightest torch you can. Place the small box inside the large box, with the torch facing the glass.

5 Close the lid of the large box and place it on a surface facing the wall. You will have to play around with the position of the large box, and of the small box inside (either backward or forward), until you get the projection you are happy with.

Enlarging templates using the grid method

As an alternative to using the homemade projector, you can use the grid method for enlarging.

Photocopy or trace your template—at the size it appears at the back of this book—on to a letter-size (A4) sheet of paper.

Mark points at ¾ in. (2 cm) intervals along the top and bottom of the sheet. Join the top and bottom points together using a pencil and ruler. Do the same on the two sides of the paper, joining the marks to make horizontal lines and forming the grid.

On the wall where you wish to place your artwork, draw grid lines

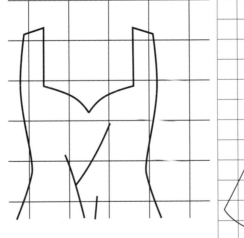

3 in. (8 cm) apart. You will probably need a triangle (set square) but you can improvise with a large NSI D-size (A1) sheet of card or a spread from a newspaper. This will give you an enlargement of 400%. Make the squares larger for an

even larger increase, or make smaller squares, like 2¼ in. (6 cm), if you do not want your image so large.

Now copy the lines in each of the small squares, scaled up into the larger squares.

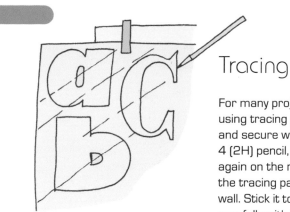

Tracing

For many projects you need to transfer the template onto paper using tracing paper. Place a sheet of tracing paper over the template and secure with some masking tape. Trace the lines with a hard 4 (2H) pencil, then turn the tracing paper over, and go over the lines again on the reverse with a softer pencil, such as a 2 (HB). Now turn the tracing paper over again and place it in position on your chosen wall. Stick it to the wall with masking tape and go over all the lines carefully with the 4 (2H) pencil, and then remove the tracing paper. This will give you a nice, clear outline.

Cutting

I use a scalpel or a craft knife for nearly all my projects. Make sure the blade is sharp and that you always use a cutting mat. When you need to make a straight cut, use a metal ruler and keep the blade in contact with the ruler at all times. Cut toward you, maintaining an even pressure.

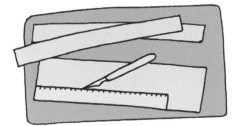

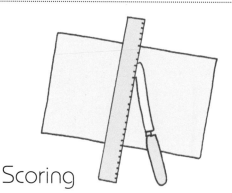

Scoring

It is important to score your paper or card stock (card) before making any fold. If it helps, you can draw a pencil line first to help you score in the right place. Place a metal ruler along the line and then score down the line, using the back (blunt) edge of a craft knife or the blunt side of a silverware (cutlery) knife. Make sure you keep the side of the blade in contact with the ruler.

Adhesives

I use different types of glue for different projects, as well as a selection of adhesive tapes. When using glue sticks, try to find one with clear glue because this type never seems to clog up. Craft (PVA) glue is white when it goes on but dries clear and is a very good adhesive for large

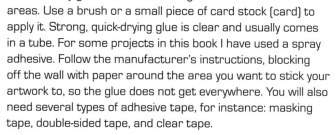

areas. Use a brush or a small piece of card stock (card) to apply it. Strong, quick-drying glue is clear and usually comes in a tube. For some projects in this book I have used a spray adhesive. Follow the manufacturer's instructions, blocking off the wall with paper around the area you want to stick your artwork to, so the glue does not get everywhere. You will also need several types of adhesive tape, for instance: masking tape, double-sided tape, and clear tape.

Stitches

RUNNING STITCH

Work from right to left. Secure the thread with a couple of small stitches, and then make several small stitches by bringing the needle up and back down through the fabric several times along the stitching line. Pull the needle through and repeat. Try to keep the stitches and the spaces between them the same size.

BACKSTITCH

Bring the needle through the fabric and take a short backward stitch on the stitching line. Bring the needle through a stitch length in front of the first stitch. Take the needle down where it first came through and repeat to sew the seam.

WHIPPED BACKSTITCH

Work a line of backstitches (see left). Using a blunt needle, slide the needle under the thread of the first backstitch from top to bottom and pull the thread through. Repeat in each stitch in the row.

BULLION KNOT

Bring the needle up at A and take it down at B, leaving a loose loop of thread—the distance from A to B being the length of knot that you require. Bring the needle back up at A and wrap the thread around the needle five to eight times, depending on how long you want the knot to be. Hold the wrapped thread in place with your left hand and pull the needle all the way through. Insert the needle at B and pull through, easing the coiled stitches neatly into position.

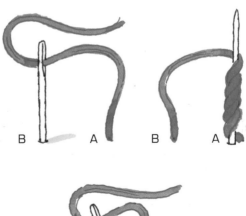

B   A   B   A

B   A

threads and stitches

Aztec wall hanging

Use fabric paint to make a striking wall hanging with natural jute or a cotton rug as your base. I have chosen bold colors for this project, to create an Aztec-style pattern formed of solid chunks of color. The result is a real statement piece. Team it up with some retro furniture and leafy plants in large pots, for a stylish, budget-friendly living area.

You will need

Template, page 139

Plain or graph paper

Pencil

Ruler

Scissors

Jute or cotton rug—mine measured 20½ x 47 in. (52 x 120 cm)

Masking tape

Flat stippling brush

Fabric paint in four colors—I chose black, pink, blue, and red

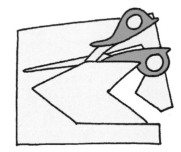

1 Enlarge the templates to the right size on a photocopier and cut them out. Alternatively, scale them up using graph paper.

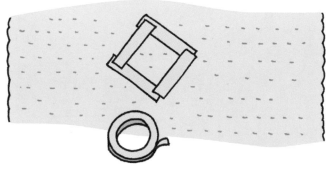

2 Find the center of your wall hanging and place the square template in position. (Fold the template into quarters in order to position it as near to the center as you can.) Lay a strip of masking tape alongside each edge of the template, pressing the tape down well.

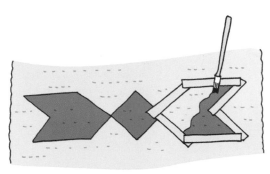

3 Remove the paper template. Use the stippling brush with a stabbing action to apply fabric paint to the area within the masking-tape border. Be sure to go into all the corners. Carefully peel off the masking tape and allow the paint to dry completely.

4 Place one of the side chevron templates in position. Follow Steps 2 and 3 to apply masking tape and stipple with paint. Continue this process with the remaining shapes.

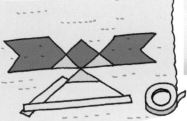

5 When applying the fabric paint, it is best to allow one area to dry completely before starting on the next. In order to keep working while this is happening, make a number of templates so that you can mask different areas that are safe to color.

6 For the squares at the top and bottom of the hanging, place two parallel rows of masking tape 1 in. (2.5 cm) apart and 2¼ in. (6 cm) in from the top and bottom edges of the hanging. Use the width of the masking tape as a guide for masking off squares and fill these in with fabric paint.

Pop color blocks

A great wall feature can be made from materials other than paper and paint. This bold set of color-block squares is made from pieced together fabric. Mix dark colors with brights and neons for a really eye-catching display. The pieced blocks are light enough to attach to the wall using sticky tack, making this a great project if you prefer not to bang nails into the wall.

You will need

8 in. (20 cm) strips of standard-width cotton in different colors

Double-sided, iron-on interfacing measuring 20 in. (50 cm)

Iron

Triangle (set square)

Ruler

Pencil

Scissors

Pins

Sewing machine

½ in. (1 cm) wide iron-on hemming tape

Sticky tack

1 Follow the instructions on the interfacing to iron it to the backs of the three different fabrics you have chosen for the large square. Use a triangle (set square), ruler, and pencil to measure and mark the rectangles and square on the back of the fabric.

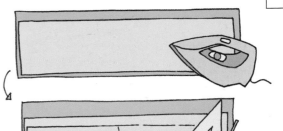

2 Cut the pieces out. Using a ruler and pencil, draw in a ½ in. (1 cm) border around the edge of each piece.

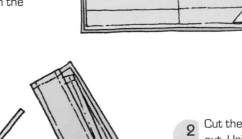

Fabric measurements

Large square:
4x 4 x 17¼ in. (10 x 44 cm)
4x 4½ x 10½ in. (11 x 27 cm)
1x 7 x 7 in. (17 x 17 cm)

Medium square:
4x 4 x 12½ in. (10 x 31.5 cm)
4x 3 x 7 in. (8 x 17 cm)
1x 4¾ x 4¾ in. (12 x 12 cm)

Small square:
4x 2¼ x 8¼ in. (6 x 21 cm)
4x 2¼ x 5 in. (6 x 13 cm)
1x 3½ x 3½ in. (9 x 9 cm)

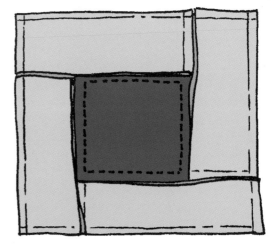

3 Lay the square over the top of one of the shorter rectangles, with right sides together and aligning their bottom right-hand corners. Pin and sew together, but only within the ½ in. (1 cm) borders you drew in Step 2. Don't sew across the ½ in. (1 cm) borders at this stage.

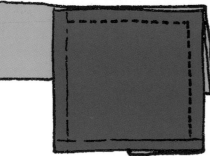

4 Pin the square to a second rectangle in the same way, aligning the top right-hand corners. This is slightly trickier, as you will have a section from the first rectangle overlapping. Tuck this out of the way for now. Pin and sew within the ½ in. (1 cm) borders.

5 Repeat Steps 3 and 4 to sew the square to the two remaining shorter rectangles. Take care to keep overlapping rectangles out of the way.

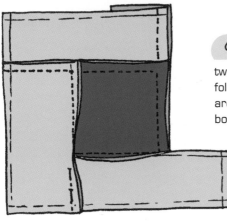

6 Now sew each corner of the square, stitching across each ½ in. (1 cm) border. This will join the two rectangles together at each corner. You need to fold back each seam where the square and rectangle are attached and position the needle at the pencil border. Sew right to the edge.

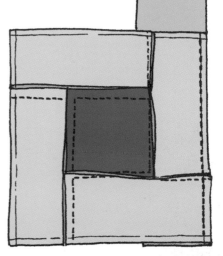

7 Follow Step 6 for each of the remaining corners.

8 Repeat Steps 3, 4, 5, and 6 to attach the larger oblong to your pieced square.

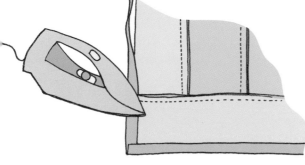

9 Press a ½ in. (1 cm) hem all around the square. Place some iron-on hemming tape inside the hem, and iron to secure.

10 Make the remaining two pieced blocks in exactly the same way. When you have made all three blocks, you can arrange them on your wall using sticky tack.

Wonderful weavings

I have a growing collection of craft books from all eras. If you open any craft book produced in the 1970s there will always be a section on weaving, complete with brightly colored tassels and hippy models. Well, weaving is back! It's cheap, easy to do, and is great fun. Use up all those little scraps of yarn you have been saving. Mix and match different colors and play around with textures by placing a chunky yarn next to the finest mohair. A group of these woven pieces hung on twigs makes a vibrant and eclectic display. Be warned: once you get started, it can become addictive!

You will need

Simple loom

Yarn (chunky and fine)

Scissors

Large darning needle

Twigs or sticks for hanging

1 Prepare the loom with warp threads. You can use woolen yarn, although I prefer to use a cotton-based knitting yarn or a thick linen thread—I find the tension holds better and there is less stretch. Tie one end of the thread around the side of the frame at the top, winding the thread around a few times first, to give you some thread to tie off with later. Slip the thread into the first notch or over the first nail and take it down to the corresponding notch or nail at the bottom. Go into this notch, or around the nail, and along to the next notch or nail. Go into or around this notch or nail and back up to the corresponding notch or nail at the top. Repeat across the entire width of the loom. Tie off the thread to the side of the frame, making sure the tension is tight.

Tip: Basic weaving terms

Warp: Threads that are held in tension across the loom.
Weft: Threads that are woven under and over the warp threads.

2 Now the fun starts! To weave back and forth in stripes, cut a length of yarn and use it to thread a darning needle. Starting from either side, weave the needle under the first warp thread and over the next, and so on across the width of the loom. Leave some yarn at the beginning for tying off later. Because there are an even number of warp threads, you always finish off on an under.

3 You will have gone under the last warp thread. Now, loop the thread back over that same warp thread, under the next, over the next, and so on until you return to where you started in Step 2. Carry on in this way, taking care not pull too tightly at the edges, as this will give your weaving an inward curve. (A loom with a metal bar avoids this problem.)

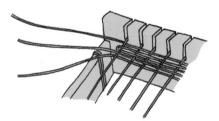

4 To change yarn, finish one color by going under the last warp thread and leaving a short length of yarn for tying off. Start off the new color in the same way that you began in Step 2, weaving under the first thread and leaving a short length of yarn to tie off.

A word on looms

You can buy a basic loom from a craft supplier. Look out for one that has a thin metal bar down each side that slots into the first and last notches. These bars are a great feature, as they help keep the weaving straight. Alternatively, make a simple loom yourself, using a wooden frame and some small nails. Mark across the top and bottom of the frame at ½ in. (1 cm) intervals, bearing in mind that you need an even number of nails at each end. If you like the idea of making smaller triangle and diamond designs, and intend to use fine wool, make the gaps smaller—say ¼ in. (6 mm). Use a small hammer to tap in the nails, leaving ½ in. (1 cm) raised.

5 Push the woven rows down as you work, so that the weave looks even. You can do this using your fingers or a fork. Store-bought looms often come with a wide comb for this purpose.

6 There are two methods for tying off. To tie off yarn that came over the warp, thread the loose length of yarn and take it through to the back of the weaving. Push the needle into the weaving, but without going through to the front. Then bring the needle up, away from the edge, and secure with a knot. To tie off yarn that came under the warp, thread it and push it down over the warp—between the two colors—and finish off in the same way.

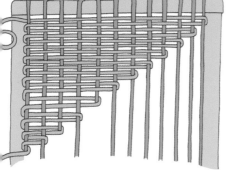

7 Use chunky yarn to weave a block made from two different-colored triangles—this is easier to work with. Weave the first triangle. Follow Step 2 to weave along the width of the loom and return. As you complete the second row, stop one thread early, so you turn on the second-to-last warp thread. Continue in this way, turning one warp thread less on each row.

8 To change color and weave the second triangle, start the new color at the opposite side from where you have finished, but at the same level. Weave across to the end and then back again.

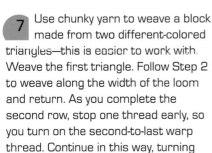

9 On the next row, when you reach the second to last warp thread go under the warp in between the woven threads of the first triangle and return back along the row.

10 Continue in this way, weaving either under or over the warp, and between the threads of the first triangle, until you have filled this area to complete the block. You may have to practice this a few times. It is worth persevering and will soon seem so simple. Once you have mastered this, you can create all sorts of designs with triangles, chevrons, and diamonds. (If using thin yarn next to chunky yarn, you will need to repeat each line twice to fill in the space.)

11 When you have finished, cut the warp ends at the bottom of the loom, leaving enough thread on each to tie off. Lift the top section of your weaving from the loom, leaving the loops intact. Cut or untie the yarn you attached at the side of the loom, thread it, and finish off at the back of the weaving, leaving a loop of similar size to the others.

12 Thread each of the warp threads at the bottom of the weaving in turn, and push through to the back of the weaving to finish off.

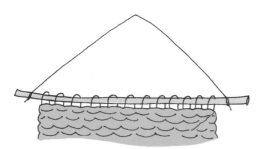

13 Thread a twig or stick through the loops at the top of the weaving and tie on a length of string at either end, for hanging.

14 Add tassels if you like. Cut some lengths of yarn measuring 8 in. (20 cm) in length. Take one, fold it in half, and thread the two ends through the needle. Bring the needle up through the weaving—from behind, and between the first and second rows at the bottom. Remove the needle and thread the two cut ends of thread though the loop. Pull gently to tighten. Continue all along and then trim—either straight across or in an arrow shape. Make a group of weavings like I have, for inspiration see the photo on page 21.

Retro chair

Stitched pieces can make wonderful and unusual works of art for framing and mounting on the wall. From tapestries to samplers, embroidered pictures have decorated walls through the decades. Stitching is very much in vogue today and is a wonderfully relaxing and enjoyable skill to learn. This stylish, retro-looking chair, with its geometric cushion, is embroidered using two simple stitches. If you are into stitching already, you may well have a number of half-used skeins of embroidery floss (thread), so what better way to use them up? Use as many colors as you want. The brighter the better!

You will need

Template, page 138

Plain or graph paper

Pencil

Light box (optional)

Masking tape

Piece of cloth measuring 18 x 22 in. (46 x 56 cm)

Air-erasable pen (optional)

Embroidery needle

Embroidery floss (thread)

Scissors

Picture frame measuring 20½ x 16½ in. (52 x 42 cm)

Clear adhesive tape

1 Enlarge the template to the right size using a photocopier. Alternatively, scale it up using graph paper.

2 If you have access to a light box, use it to trace the image onto the cloth. If not, use masking tape to stick the template to a window, position the cloth over the template, and draw the design onto the cloth. You can use an air-erasable pen or a pencil, as you will be covering all the lines with stitches. Position the image on the cloth, 5½ in. (14 cm) up from the bottom edge and centered between the two side edges.

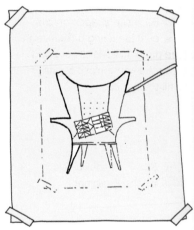

3 Follow the stitch guide, using backstitch (see page 11) to embroider the outline of the chair.

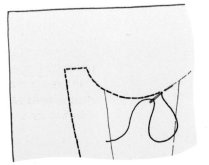

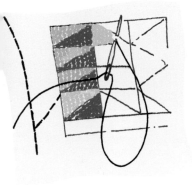

 4 Fill in the shapes on the cushion using bullion knots (see page 11). Make sure you place the knots close together to fill the space.

5 Stitch the bullion knots on the chair back.

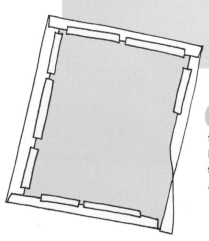

6 Stretch the cloth across the backing board from the picture frame, with an even border all around. Fold the overlapping edges over to the back and secure with some clear adhesive tape.

Cute Kitty appliqué

I recently bought a little stash of hand-dyed woolen fabrics—tiny pieces in a wonderful selection of colors. I knew I wanted to use them to make a wall hanging with a retro feel to it. At home, I had an old cotton-knit sweater that was heading for the recycling. It was a lovely bright-green color—the purr-fect background for the flowers on this stylish kitty.

You will need

Fine cotton-knit fabric measuring 21¾ x 12 in. (55 x 30 cm)

Double-sided, iron-on interfacing measuring 21¾ x 17¾ in. (55 x 45 cm)

Iron

Templates, page 141

Plain or graph paper

Pencil

Masking tape

Scissors

Pins

Felted wool measuring 16 x 24¾ in. (40 x 63 cm)

Air-erasable pen

Sewing machine

Sewing thread in different colors

Scraps of fabric in different colors

¾ in. (2 cm) wide iron-on hemming tape

Length of doweling measuring 17 x ¼ in. (43 x 0.6 cm)

String

1 Follow the manufacturer's instructions to iron the interfacing to the back of the fabric you are using for the body of the cat. Don't peel off the backing paper yet.

2 Enlarge the template for the cat to the right size using a photocopier. Alternatively, scale it up using graph paper. It is quite big, so you will have to do this in sections, sticking them together with masking tape. Cut the cat shape out and pin it to the right side of the fabric. Draw around the shape and cut it out.

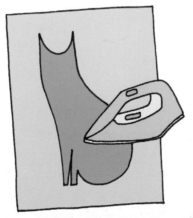

3 Peel off the backing paper on the interfacing, position the body of the cat on the felted wool, placing it 2¼ in. (6 cm) up from the bottom and centered between the two side edges. Iron the shape in place.

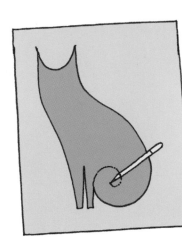

4 Use an air-erasable pen to draw in the spiral for the tail following the design on the template. Set your sewing machine to a close zigzag stitch and sew all around the edge of the cat, stitching over the line drawn in for the tail. I used a green-color thread, but use a contrasting color if you prefer.

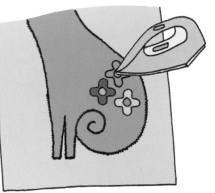

5 Iron interfacing to the different scraps of fabrics you have chosen for the flowers. Trace out the templates for the two different-sized flowers and their centers. Pin the templates to the fabrics and cut out three of the larger flowers and three of the smaller size.

6 Arrange the flowers on the cat. Peel the backing paper from the interfacing and iron the flowers in place. Repeat with the centers of all the flowers.

7 Use zigzag stitch to sew around the outlines of the flowers and their centers. I like to match the color of the thread to the fabric, but you don't have to.

8 Repeat steps 5, 6, and 7 to sew on the cat's eyes and nose.

9 Use an air-erasable pen to draw in the mouth and the whiskers following the design on the template. Stitch these in using a zigzag stitch.

10 Turn over a ¾ in. (2 cm) hem along the bottom and two side edges of the felted wool. Press, then place hemming tape within the folded hems and press again to secure.

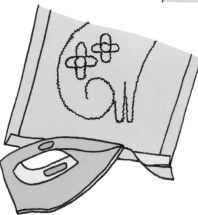

11 Fold over a 1 in. (2.5 cm) hem along the top edge of the felted wool. Pin and sew a line of stitching, making sure you leave a gap for the doweling. Insert the doweling into the hem and tie some string around each end for hanging.

Cactus-pot prints

This project involves making simple stencils and overprinting them using stamps made from erasers. I have printed my fun little cactus pictures on calico cotton, which I have then stitched onto some patterned card stock (card) to give them jazzy little frames!

You will need

Calico cotton

Scissors

Tape measure

Templates, page 138

Tracing paper

Masking tape

Pencil

Thin paper

Craft knife

Cutting mat

Erasers

Ink-stamping pad

Posterboard (cardboard)

Thin card stock (card) in different colors or patterns

Fabric glue

Sewing machine

1 Cut several pieces of calico cotton measuring 5 x 7 in. (13 x 18 cm).

2 Trace the templates and transfer them to thin paper.

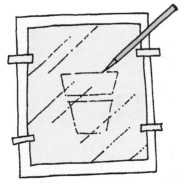

3 Using a craft knife, and protecting your work surface with a cutting mat, cut out the shapes to make your stencils. Do not throw away the cut-out section for the flowerpot base.

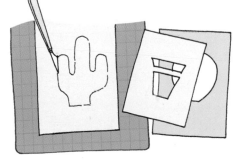

4 Position the stencil for the flowerpot toward the lower section of a piece of calico and centered between the two sides. Secure with masking tape.

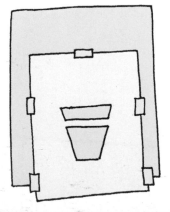

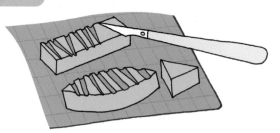

5 Cut a number of different shapes from the erasers—lines or circles—using a craft knife.

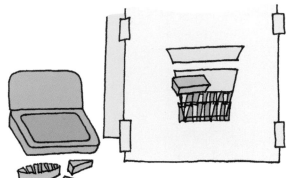

6 Use the erasers to print into the stencil, making sure you go right into all the corners. Experiment by using two different colors—you will get some lovely textural effects. Remove the stencil to reveal a colorful flowerpot with nice crisp edges. Leave it to dry.

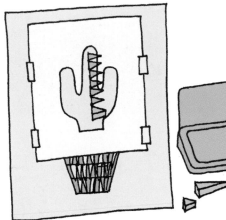

7 Position one of the cacti shapes above the flowerpot, aligning the bottom of the cactus with the top of the flowerpot. Secure with masking tape. Use the erasers to print into the stencil. Simple triangles printed in rows work well to represent the ridged surface of a cactus.

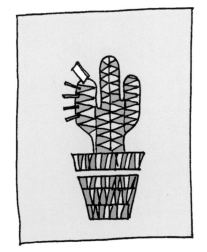

8 Cut a small piece of posterboard (cardboard) and, using just the edge, print prickles on the cactus.

9 For the cactus made using oval shapes, cut an eraser to this shape and score in the same way. Use a small piece of posterboard (cardboard) to print the flowers.

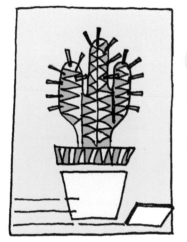

10 Mask your stenciled flowerpot base using the cut-out paper shape that you saved in Step 3. Using the edge of a piece posterboard (cardboard), print a grid shape for the tablecloth.

11 Cut some rectangles of card stock (card) making sure they are bigger than the pieces of calico by ¾ in. (2 cm) all around.

12 Use fabric glue to stick the calico pieces to the card stock (card). Machine-stitch around all four edges to finish.

Beautiful beastie

I have made this handsome beastie wall hanging from natural felted wool and linen. By restricting the color pallete to a dark, charcoal gray and natural tones I have created a striking finish and one that would look great on its own or with a collection of black-and-white pictures on a gallery wall.

1 Start by painting five white circles on the linen. Make them approximately 3 in. (8 cm) in diameter. Don't worry if they are not perfect circles, or if the paint doesn't cover the linen completely, as this gives added character and texture.

2 Iron double-sided interfacing onto the back of the painted linen and cut out squares measuring 4¾ in. (12 cm) square, each with a painted circle at the center. Don't peel the backing paper off yet.

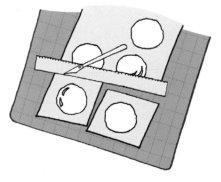

You will need

Linen measuring 16 x 10 in. (40 x 25 cm)

White fabric paint

Paintbrush

Double-sided, iron-on interfacing measuring 16 x 10 in. (40 x 25 cm)

Iron

Craft knife

Cutting mat

Ruler

Templates, page 138

Tracing paper

Masking tape

Pencil

Pins

Felted wool measuring 30 x 12 in. (75 x 30 cm)

Embroidery needle

Embroidery floss (thread) in white and charcoal gray

Dressmaker's pencil in a pale color

2 lengths of linen tape, each measuring 4 in. (10 cm)

Sewing machine

Balsa wood measuring 12 x 1 x ¼ in. (30 x 2.5 x 0.6 cm)

Washi tape

Awl (bradawl), or similar, for making smaller holes

String

3 Enlarge and trace out the shapes for the templates and cut them out. Pin the templates to the painted linen, positioning them over the circles, as shown, so that they become part of the design. Cut out all the different shapes.

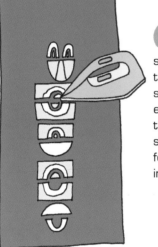

4 Position the shapes on the felted wool, as shown, starting 2 in. (5 cm) up from the bottom and centering the shapes between the two side edges. Piece by piece, remove the backing paper from the shapes and iron in place following the manufacturer's instructions for the interfacing.

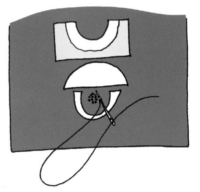

5 Thread the embroidery needle with white floss (thread) and use bullion knots (see page 11) to stitch in the designs. Start at the tail end stitch a group of knots to make a circle.

6 On the fifth shape up from the bottom, stitch a row of charcoal-gray bullion knots around the painted semicircle and stitch a row of white bullion knots around the semicircle above that. Still using white floss (thread), sew a number of straight stitches between the eighth and ninth shapes. Now stitch a row of charcoal-gray knots around the semicircle on the twelfth shape. Stitch white knots around the two eyes. Use charcoal-gray floss (thread) to stitch some backstitch lines (see page 11) across the face section.

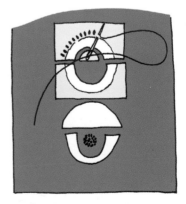

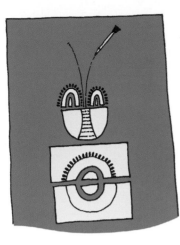

7 Use a dressmaker's pencil to draw in the antennae. You need a gap of at least 2 in. (5 cm) between the top of the antennae and the top of the felted wool. Stitch these in white floss (thread) using whipped backstitch (see page 11). Finish with a white bullion knot at the top of each antenna.

8 Using the leg template as a guide, draw in the legs with the dressmaker's pencil. Stitch the legs in white floss (thread) using a whipped backstitch and finish each with a bullion knot.

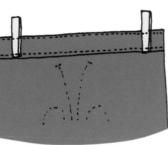

9 Turn over a 1 in. (2.5 cm) hem at the top of the felted wool and pin in place. Fold each length of linen tape in half and pin to the back of the hem, positioning each 1 in. (2.5 cm) in from each edge and overlapping the hem by a few millimeters. Use a sewing machine to stitch along the bottom of the hem, then across the top of the hem, close to the edge.

10 Cover the balsa wood with washi tape. I used a black-and-white stripe to keep in with the color theme.

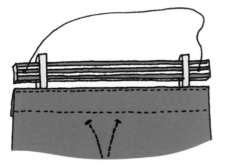

11 At each end of the balsa wood, use an awl (bradawl) to make a hole ¾ in. (2 cm) in from the edge. Slot the balsa wood through the linen loops and thread some string through each hole for hanging.

Macramé wall hanging

Macramé is back! In the 1970s, macramé was everywhere: You hung your plants in baskets made from it, you wore macramé belts, bracelets, and necklaces, and you placed your bits and pieces in long-handled bags made from knotted string. The vintage craft books that I've been collecting recently all have a section on this forgotten craft, so I grabbed a length of doweling and some string, and set about learning how to do it. Basically, there are just two important knots that you need to learn in order to create wonderful wall hangings.

You will need

¾ in. (2 cm) wooden baton measuring 40 in. (1 m)

110 yd. (100 m) of ¼ in. (8 mm) rope

Tape measure

Scissors

Small hacksaw

1 Cut 16 lengths of rope measuring 5 yd. (4.5 m). Fold each length in half and hold the loop in front of the wooden baton. Fold the loop over to the back of the baton, and thread the ends of the rope through the loop to secure, as shown. Attach all lengths of rope to the baton in this way.

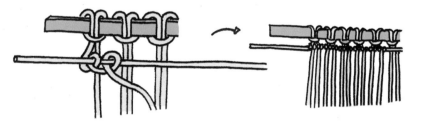

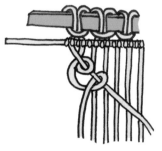

2 Cut a length of rope measuring 40 in. (1 m). Lay it horizontally across the rope lengths you tied in Step 1, just below the knots. Keeping the horizontal strand taut, and working from left to right, follow the diagrams to make a half hitch knot followed by a double half hitch knot with each of the vertical strands—all the way along the horizontal strand. Keep the knots close and even to make a neat row. (You will have a rope end sticking out to each side, but you can neaten those off later.)

3 Working from the left, take the first vertical strand and hold it diagonally to the right over the next few strands. Take the second vertical strand and form a double half hitch on the diagonal strand.

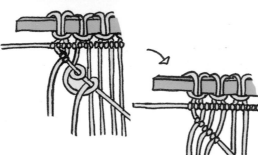

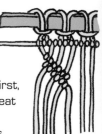

4 Take the third vertical strand and form a second double half hitch on the diagonal strand. Repeat with the fourth vertical strand.

5 Still working on the first, diagonal strand, repeat Steps 3 and 4 to make a second row of half hitches.

6 Repeat Steps 3, 4, and 5 on the remaining groups of four strands. In each case, the 5th, 9th, 13th, 17th, 21st, 25th, and 29th vertical strands will become the diagonal strands on which the knots are made.

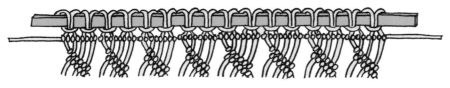

7 Repeat Step 2, using a new 40 in. (1 m) length of rope, and placing it just below the knots you made in Step 6

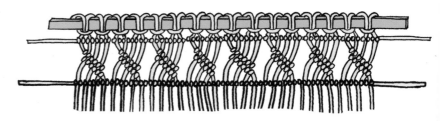

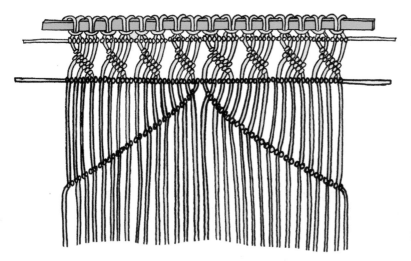

8 Working at the center of the wall hanging, take the 16th vertical strand and hold it diagonally to the left. Take the 15th vertical strand and make a double half hitch knot on the diagonal strand, just as you did in Step 3. Continue to work toward the left of the wall hanging, making double half hitch knots using strands 14, 13, 12, and so on, until you reach the end.

9 Repeat Step 8, taking the 17th vertical strand diagonally to the right.

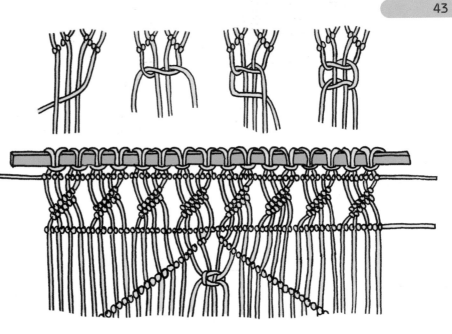

10 Now work on the four strands at the center of the wall hanging and follow the diagrams to complete a square knot 2 in. (5 cm) below where the diagonals you made in Steps 8 and 9 meet. Try to keep the knot flat and even.

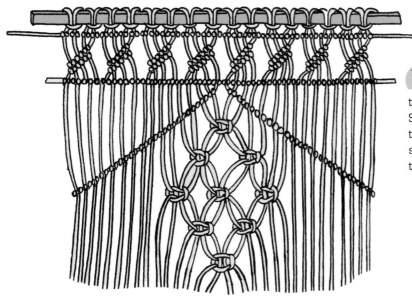

11 Take the two left-hand strands emerging from the square knot you made in Step 10, and the two strands to the left of these. Make a second square knot 1 in. (3 cm) lower than the first square knot.

12 Repeat Step 11 using the two right-hand strands emerging from the square knot you made in Step 10, and the two strands to the right of these.

13 Take the center four strands emerging from the square knots you made in Steps 11 and 12. Make a square knot 1 in. (3 cm) lower down.

14 Take the four strands to the left of the central knot and make a square knot at the same level.

15 Take the four strands to the right of the central knot and make a square knot at the same level. You should now have three knots in a row.

16 Repeat Steps 11 and 12 to make a row of two square knots below the row of three and make a final square knot beneath that. You should now have a diamond shape formed of square knots.

17 Take the first vertical strand on the left and, holding it diagonally, repeat Step 8, working from left to right, to make double half hitch knots up to strand 15.

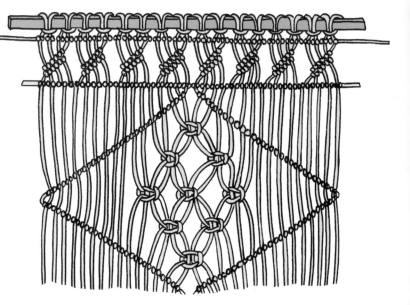

18 Repeat Step 17 using the 32nd vertical strand and working from right to left. You will have completed a diamond shape around the square knots.

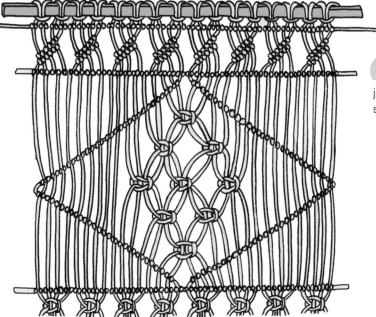

19 Repeat Step 2, using a new 40 in. (1 m) length of rope, and placing it just below the lowest point of the diamond shape you completed in Step 18.

20 Make square knots across the width of the wall hanging, using groups of four vertical strands, as before. Make the knots 2 in. (5 cm) below the horizontal bar. Try to keep the knots even and at the same level.

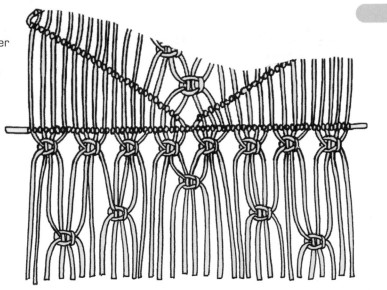

21 Take the four strands at the center of the wall hanging, and make a square knot 1 in. (3 cm) below the row of square knots you made in Step 20.

22 Take strands 8, 9, 10, 11 and make a square knot 4 in. (10 cm) below the row of square knots you made in Step 20.

23 Repeat Step 22 on the right-hand side using strands 22, 23, 24, and 25.

24 Repeat Step 22 using strands 3, 4, 5, and 6 and 27, 28, 29, and 30 to make two more square knots. Position them 2¾ in. (7 cm) below the knots you made in Steps 22 and 23.

25 Trim the vertical strands of rope so that they hang evenly, 8 in. (20 cm) below the knots you made in Step 24.

26 Turn the wall hanging over and poke any spare ends of rope emerging from the horizontal bars into the backs of the knots. Use a hacksaw to trim the wooden baton, leaving 1 in. (3 cm) either side of the rope.

Tips

- This wall hanging measures 5¼ x 2 ft. (160 x 60 cm) and uses a lot of rope! If you want a smaller wall hanging, use cotton washing-line rope, which is thinner.
- You don't have to use rope until you make your main piece. I suggest you practice making the double half hitches and square knots again and again using eight strands on a length of doweling, until you can do them neatly and evenly. If you use string, you will make the wall hanging in mini form.
- Note that all macramé is worked in groups of four strands so you must always have multiples of four.

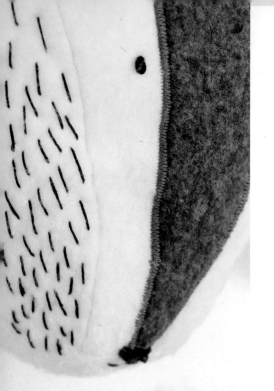

Furry friends trophy heads

Trophy heads come in all shapes and sizes and can be made using many different materials, including card stock (card), wood, or papier-mâché. These cute little creatures are made of fabric and add a fun element to any child's bedroom. The base pattern is the same for each little character—just customize it as you like to create your own unique menagerie! The instructions that follow are for the white trophy head.

You will need

Templates, page 138

Paper or graph paper

Pencil

Scissors

Fabric, such as soft felted wools, in different colors

Pins

Sewing machine

Fiberfill (toy stuffing)

Embroidery needle

Embroidery floss (thread)

Cotton tape

1 Enlarge the templates to the right size on a photocopier or scale them up using graph paper. Cut out the shapes.

2 With right sides facing, fold in half the fabric you have chosen for the main part of the head. Position the template for the ear and the side sections on the fabric and pin in place. Cut around the templates to make two side sections and two ear sections.

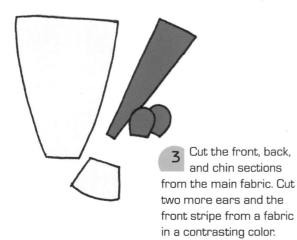

3 Cut the front, back, and chin sections from the main fabric. Cut two more ears and the front stripe from a fabric in a contrasting color.

4 Work on the front of the head. Center the front stripe over the front section, with both pieces right side up and aligning the straight edges at the top. Pin in position, set your sewing machine to a close zigzag, and sew down each side of the front stripe.

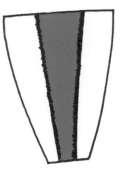

5 Take two ear sections—one of each color—and pin them together, right sides facing. Sew a ¼ in. (6 mm) seam around the curved section. Leave the bottom, straight section, open. Trim the seam back to ⅛ in. (3 mm) and turn the right way out. Repeat to make the second ear.

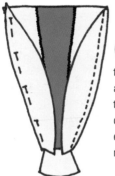

6 With right sides facing, pin and sew the short, straight edge (opposite the curved edge) of the chin section to the bottom edge of the front section.

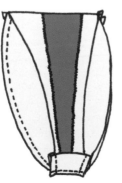

7 Taking one of the side sections (follow the template to note inside and outside edges), align its inside edge with the corresponding edge of the front section, right sides facing, and so that the pointed end of the side panel is at the top. Pin the two sections together. The two pieces curve in opposite directions, so ease the fabric together as you work—this is easier to do if the fabric has a bit of stretch to it. Sew and repeat on the other side of the face.

8 With right sides facing, align the bottom straight edge of one side section with the side edge of the chin section. Pin, sew, and repeat on the other side.

9 Make a small pleat along the straight edge of each ear and pin both to the front section so that the straight edges align with the top edge of the front section, as shown. Align the outside edge of each ear with the seam sewn for the side section. Tack in place using a couple of big stitches and remove the pins.

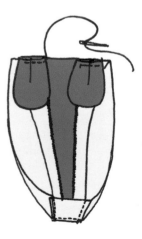

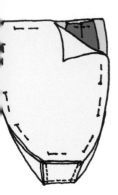

10 With right sides facing, pin the back section to the front section. Sew a ¼ in. (6 mm) seam all around, leaving a 2¼ in. (6 cm) gap in the side seam.

11 Turn the head the right way out and stuff with some fiberfill (toy stuffing). Turn in the raw ends at the gap, pin, and close the gap using small stitches.

12 Using an embroidery needle and floss (thread), sew a bullion knot for each eye (see page 11). Sew three bullion knots close together for the nose and sew an upside down "T" shape in straight stitches for the mouth.

13 Sew some long, straight stitches on the side sections. Start them quite close together at the bottom of the head and fan them out toward the top.

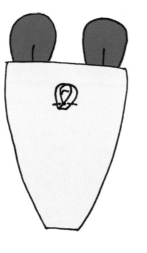

14 Cut a 2 in. (5 cm) length of cotton tape. Fold it in half to make a loop and stitch it to the back of the head, centrally and 2 in. (5 cm) from the top, for hanging.

Tip

Customize the heads in different ways. I made some sections using a third color/fabric. I also added bullion knots to the front of one head for extra texture. You can change the shapes of the ears and sew the side stitches in two or three contrasting colors.

cuts and folds

Folded arrowheads

You can make a stylish artwork simply by using pieces of card stock (card) and a frame. Here, I have arranged a number of 3-D triangles in columns to create a contemporary, graphic look. The subtle variations in color and shadows cast from the points of the triangles add an extra dimension and interest.

You will need

Template, page 139

Plain or graph paper

Tracing paper

Masking tape

Pencil

Thin card stock (card) in different colors

Craft knife

Cutting mat

Blunt knife, or similar, for scoring

Craft (PVA) glue

Large sheet of foamboard 20 x 27½ in. (50 x 70 cm) frame

Ruler

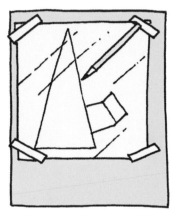

1 Enlarge the triangle template to the right size using a photocopier. Alternatively, scale it up using graph paper. Trace the template and transfer on to colored card stock (card).

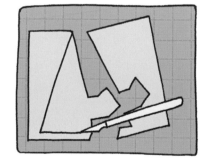

2 Using a craft knife, and protecting your work surface with a cutting mat, cut out the shape.

3 Use a blunt knife to score the folds marked on the template.

4 Fold the shape to make a 3-D triangle. Run craft (PVA) glue along the flap and stick in place. This will hold the triangle in shape. Follow Steps 1 to 4 to make 24 shapes in total.

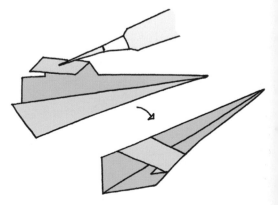

5 Cut the foamboard to the same dimensions as your frame. Draw in a light pencil line, ¾ in. (2 cm) in from the left-hand side of the card and from top to bottom.

6 Stick down the first triangle, placing the wide end on the pencil line, 2¾ in. (7 cm) down from the top of the foamboard.

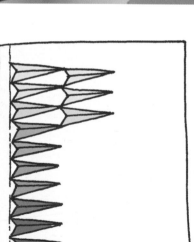

7 Stick more triangles directly below the first, with the wide ends touching, as shown. Stick a second column of triangles in position, so that the wide ends of these triangles span between two points of triangles in the first column.

8 Continue to build the pattern— either following mine, or to match a design of your own.

9 Once all the triangles are in place, use an eraser to rub out any pencil lines still showing. Remove the glass from the frame and replace with your foamboard artwork.

Pretty patchwork

This project couldn't be simpler and looks gorgeous on a bedroom wall. I have used a mix of florals and geometrics in a pallete of bright, vibrant colors, using old bits of giftwrap, scraps of wallpaper, and even a section of script typography torn from an old magazine. This is a project that you can easily adapt. Mix geometric patterns with sections cut from old comics, add more typography for a graphic and contemporary look, or mix in sections cut from the kids' paintings and drawings.

You will need

Templates, page 139

Plain or graph paper

Tracing paper

Masking tape

Pencil

Thin card stock (card)

Craft knife

Cutting mat

Scraps of paper

Ruler

Craft (PVA) glue

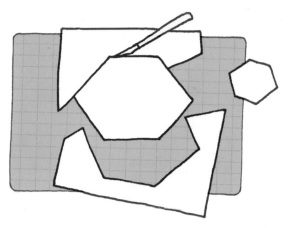

1 Enlarge the hexagon templates to the right size using a photocopier. Alternatively, scale them up using graph paper. Trace the templates, transfer them to card stock (card), and cut them out. Use a craft knife and protect your work surface with a cutting mat

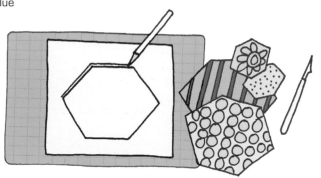

2 Draw around each card template on the backs of different plain and patterned scraps of paper.

Cut out your hexagons using a ruler and craft knife for nice crisp edges.

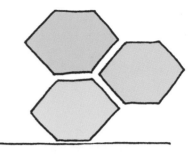

4 Start assembling your patchwork on the wall. Take each the large hexagon, spread glue over the back, and position it on the wall. Align the bottom edge of the hexagon with the straight edge of the baseboard (skirting board).

5 Continue until you have stuck down all of your large hexagons, keeping an even gap of ¼ in. (8 mm) between each one.

6 To complete the patchwork, stick some of the smaller hexagons onto the larger ones, centering them by eye. You don't have to put a smaller shape on all of the large ones. It is quite nice to vary it.

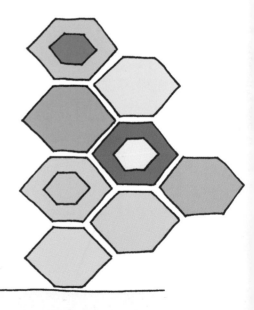

Galloping horses

These unusual and colorful posterboard (cardboard) horses make a delightful decoration for a child's bedroom wall. Not only do they look fantastic, they have the added wow factor of galloping at the pull a string! Based on old-fashioned, jumping jack toys, my use of bright, graphic prints gives these horses a contemporary twist.

You will need

Templates, page 141

Plain or graph paper

Tracing paper

Pencil

Masking tape

Thin card stock (card)

Craft knife

Cutting mat

Craft (PVA) glue

Patterned paper

Awl (bradawl) or similar

Scissors

Split pins

String or waxed cotton thread

1 Enlarge the templates for all the body parts of the horse to the right size using a photocopier. Alternatively, scale them up using graph paper. Trace them out and transfer them to card stock (card). Use a craft knife to cut them out, protecting your work surface with a cutting mat.

2 Spread glue over the front of the main body of the horse (excluding the tail—you will cover this piece in Step 4) and stick it to the wrong side of some patterned paper. Position the shape in such a way that the tail hangs over the edge of the paper, and so won't be covered in paper. Smooth down to stick evenly. Using a craft knife on a cutting mat, cut all around the edge of the body to remove any excess paper. Take care not to cut off the tail.

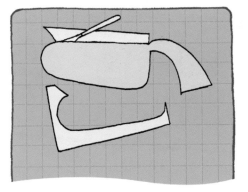

3 Repeat Step 2 to cover and cut out the head and the leg sections of the horse.

4 Now you can cover the tail section. Spread glue on the right side, turn it over, and position it on the wrong side of some patterned paper. This time make sure the horse's body overlaps the edge and so won't be covered. Trim off the excess paper.

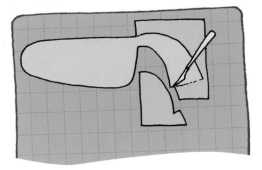

5 Trace out the shapes for the saddle, mane, eye, and head pieces, and transfer them to patterned paper. Cut out each shape and glue in position on the horse.

6 Follow the guides on the templates to make holes in the body and legs. Use an awl (bradawl) or similar.

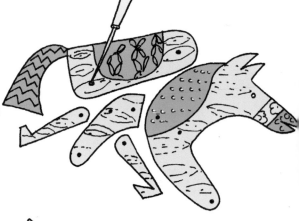

7 Assemble the horse. Start by pushing a pin through the hole in the head section—from the back to the front—and opening the pin to lay flush on the front of the piece. Repeat with the front leg section, pushing the pin through the hole at the top of the leg.

8 Push a pin through the hole at the top of the back leg section in the same way.

9 Use pins to join the lower legs to the upper legs. This time, push the pin through from the front of the horse so that the pin opens up at the back.

10 Follow Step 9 to join the head and front leg section together, and the back leg section to the main body in the same way.

11 Cut a length of string or waxed cotton measuring 10 in (25 cm). Tie each end around one pin at the back of the horse. This joins the head and front leg section to the back leg section.

12 Cut a length of string measuring 12 in. (30 cm). Tie one end around the middle of the loop going from the front to the back legs. Secure it at the middle with a knot and let the rest hang down.

Elegant swan

The traditional art of paper cutting has been practiced all over the world for many centuries, each region having developed it's own unique styles and techniques. In recent years, the art has become popular in the world of contemporary craft and design, with many paper artists producing stunningly creative pieces. With a little patience and careful cutting, you can produce a beautiful work using the method described here. This graceful swan design is worked in three sections and is mounted in a box frame to give an unusual 3-D effect.

You will need

Templates, page 140

Tracing paper

Pencil

Masking tape

White cartridge paper

Craft knife

Cutting mat

Colored paper (orange, green, and blue)

Spray adhesive

Face mask

Blunt knife, or similar, for scoring

Craft (PVA) glue

Box frame measuring 10 x 10 x 1 ½ in. (25 x 25 x 3.5 cm)

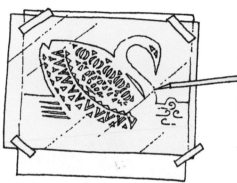

1 Enlarge the swan template to the right size using a photocopier. Alternatively, scale it up using graph paper. Trace the template, turn the trace over and transfer it on to white cartridge paper. This is the reverse side of the swan.

2 Using a craft knife, and protecting your work surface with a cutting mat, cut away the design. Follow the template closely to make sure you cut away the right sections.

3 Use the template to cut the orange paper section of the swan. Apply a thin coat of spray adhesive to the back of the white swan and place the white swan over the orange swan. Always follow the manufacturer's instructions when using this spray adhesive—you should wear a mask. Cut away the section between the swan's neck and its body, and trim any pieces of orange paper that are sticking out of place.

4 Enlarge the leaf section teamplate and trace it out, turn the trace over and transfer it on to white cartridge paper. Cut out the design.

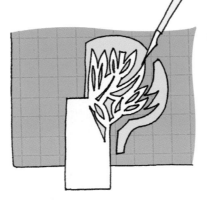

5 Cut a piece of green paper that is larger than the area of paper-cut leaves. Apply a thin coat of spray adhesive to the back of the leaf section and place it over the green paper, making sure that all the cut-out sections are covered by the colored paper. Using a craft knife, trim any excess green paper around the edges.

6 Enlarge and trace out the template for the cloud section. Turn the trace over and transfer the design on to the back of a piece of white cartridge paper measuring 10 x 10 in. (25 x 25 cm). Cut out the design.

7 Cut out a piece of blue paper measuring 10 x 10 in. (25 x 25 cm). Apply a thin coat of spray adhesive to the back of the white section and place it over the blue section, aligning all the edges.

8 Use a blunt knife to score the two side edges of the swan section—follow the template as a guide. Fold the two side edges back and dab some craft glue down each side.

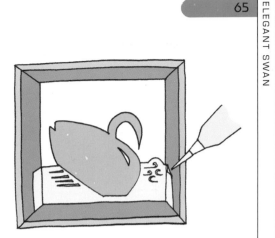

9 Position the swan inside the back of the box frame along the bottom. Stick the two side edges to the sides of the box frame, making sure that the swan is pushed as far forward within the frame as it will go.

10 Following the template as a guide, score down the side flap of the leaf section. Fold it back and dab some craft (PVA) glue on the flap. Stick this to the left side of the box frame, positioning it approximately ½ in. (1 cm) back from the swan section.

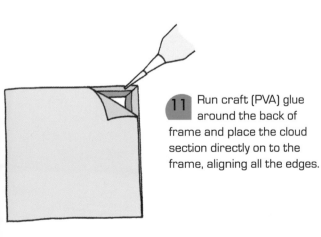

11 Run craft (PVA) glue around the back of frame and place the cloud section directly on to the frame, aligning all the edges.

Shimmering firefly

I have always loved Chinese kites made from brightly colored tissue paper in the shapes of birds or dragons. They are the inspiration behind this magnificent creature. I used beautiful, vibrant Chinese paper in gold, silver, and orange—you can buy it in Chinese supermarkets. If you can't get hold of Chinese paper, use any orange, gold, and silver paper or thin card stock (card). It will have the same effect.

You will need

Templates, page 142

Plain or graph paper

Pencil

Masking tape

Scissors

Foamboard

Craft knife

Cutting mat

Tracing paper

Thin card stock (card)

Orange, gold, and silver paper or thin card stock (card)

Craft (PVA) glue

Strong, quick-drying glue

Ruler

Blunt knife, or similar, for scoring

1 Enlarge the wing templates to the right size using a photocopier. Alternatively, scale them up using graph paper. The artwork is quite big, so you will have to do this in sections, sticking them together with masking tape. Cut the templates out. Lay them on the foamboard, secure with some masking tape, and draw around them.

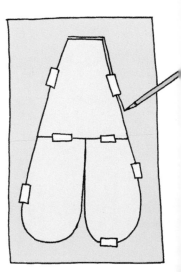

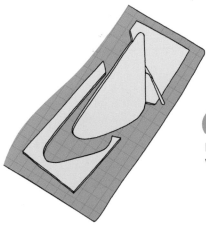

2 Cut out the shapes. Use a craft knife and protect your work surface with a cutting mat.

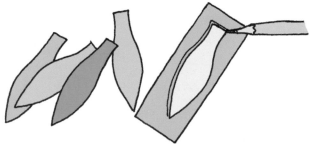

3 Enlarge the template for the colored paper parts, then trace and transfer it to a piece of thin card stock (card). Use this template to cut out lots of shapes. I used mainly gold and orange for the outer wings and silver for the inner wings.

4 Start covering the outer wings with colored shapes. Taking each shape in turn, fold it in half to make a crease down the center. Dab a little craft (PVA) glue on the back of the top section and stick it down at the top of a wing.

5 Stick the shapes down in rows, overlapping them so that the glued ends are tucked in under the shapes above them.

6 Continue to stick the shapes on all the wing shapes. For the inner wings, note that you don't have to cover the whole of the foamboard as you will be sticking the body in the center of the silver wings, and the gold wings will overlap the silver wings a little on the outer edges (use the photo on the previous page as a guide).

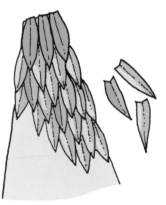

7 Spread some strong, quick-drying glue over the uncovered sections of the inner wings. Place the outer wing sections over the inner wings, aligning the two at the top. Make sure the outer wings spread out to reveal the silver wings below.

8 Enlarge the template for the body section and use this to cut the shape from thin card stock (card). Use the templates for the eyes to make the shapes from colored paper and stick them in position. I also cut rectangles of colored paper to decorate the body.

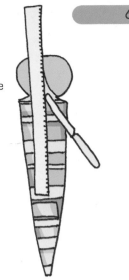

9 Use a ruler and a blunt knife to score down the center of the body section and fold to make a crease.

10 Spread glue on the back of the body section, just below the head. Stick it in position, aligning the top of the body with the top of the wings.

11 Cut two strips of thin card stock (card) measuring ½ x 16 in. (1 x 40 cm). Wind each strip around a pencil to make a coil.

12 Cut a slit in the bottom edge of each coil—it must be very thin. Cut two thin slits in the top of the head, ½ in. (1 cm) either side of the central fold. Slip the paper coils into the slits in the head to make the antennae. If they are too loose, add a dab of glue to secure.

Stylish paper art

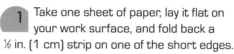

Sometimes something as ordinary as a folded sheet of white paper can contribute to a unique piece of art simply by the way you group and display it. This project is easy but also, I think, beautiful in a stylish and elegant way.

You will need

20 sheets white paper measuring 3½ x 5½ in. (9 x 14 cm)

Scissors

Craft glue

Thin string or embroidery floss (thread)

Large sharp needle

Masking tape

Box frame measuring 10 x 10 in. (25 x 25 cm)

Thin white card stock (card)

1 Take one sheet of paper, lay it flat on your work surface, and fold back a ½ in. (1 cm) strip on one of the short edges.

2 Turn the paper over and repeat the fold in the opposite direction. Continue in this way until you have made a concertina. Trim any excess paper to the last complete folded strip.

3 Fold the concertina in half lengthways. Spread glue on one of the central folds, as shown, and stick the two sides together to make a fan shape.

4 Repeat Steps 1 to 3 to make 20 fans in total.

5 Cut some lengths of thin string or embroidery floss (thread). Thread the needle and poke it through the bottom of a fan. Use glue to secure the string in the dip of one of the fan's folds, and thread a second fan in the same way.

6 String five fans together and repeat the process three more times to make four groups of five fans.

7 Using masking tape, secure the two ends of each length of string to the inside of the box frame—one at the top and one at the bottom—so that each line of fans is suspended within the frame. Start at the left side of the frame and work your way across. You can choose if you want them all to be the same way up, or to alternate right and wrong way up (see photo above).

8 Cut two strips of white card stock (card) to run along the inside edges at the top and bottom of the box frame. Glue these strips in place, pressing them down over the ends of the strings held with masking tape. (Pull the strings taut before pressing down the card firmly to secure.) Trim any excess string.

Shadow box

Create this enchanting scene using tiers of cut paper held within a wooden frame. Switch on the light to illuminate the little scene and to set the sky alight with twinkling stars.

You will need

Wood measuring 40 x 2¾ x ½ in. (100 x 6.8 x 1.2 cm)

Wood saw

Hammer

Panel pins

Wood glue

White paint

Paintbrush

Templates, page 143

Plain or graph paper

Pencil

Tracing paper

Masking tape

White cartridge paper

Craft knife

Cutting mat

Ruler

Blunt knife, or similar, for scoring

Craft (PVA) glue

Thick gray paper

Hole punch with a ⅛ in. (3 mm) punch

String of battery-operated LED fairy lights

Thin gray card stock (card) measuring 9½ x 9½ in. (24 x 24 cm)

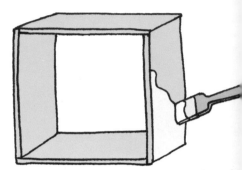

1 Follow the instructions on page 101 to make the wooden frame measuring 9½ x 9½ in. (24 x 24 cm). Paint the frame white.

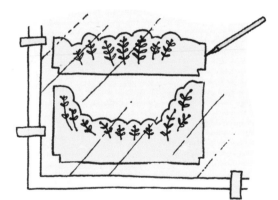

2 Enlarge the foliage templates to the right size on a photocopier. Alternatively, scale them up using graph paper. Use a pencil to trace the shapes out, turn the trace over onto a sheet of white cartridge paper, and go over the lines.

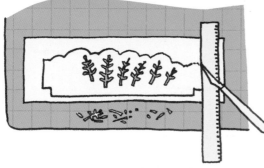

3 Follow the pencil lines to cut out the shapes, using a craft knife and protecting your work surface with a cutting mat. Use a ruler for any straight edges.

4 Follow the templates, and use a blunt knife to score where indicated and fold the gluing edges back.

5 Place piece A within the frame, making sure it fits snugly. (If it doesn't, slightly adjust the width of the flaps.) Dab glue on all folded edges and position within the frame so that it is flush with the front.

6 Stick piece B within the frame, aligning the front of it with the back edge of the glued tab on piece A, a gap of ⅛ in. (8 mm).

7 Repeat Step 6 with pieces C, D, and E, each time with a ¼ in. (8 mm) gap between them.

8 Enlarge and trace out the template for the row of houses. Turn the trace over onto a sheet of white cartridge paper, and go over the lines in pencil. Cut the shapes out.

9 Enlarge and trace out the template for the sky section. Turn the trace over onto a sheet of gray paper, and go over the lines in pencil. Score the lines where indicated. Cut out the stars and use the hole punch to make holes all along the lines for the trails of stars. Leave a couple of millimeters between each hole.

10 Glue the row of houses to the gray paper, aligning the base of the house section with the bottom fold of the gray paper. Use the windows in the houses as a guide to cut windows from the gray paper. Fold the tabs along the score lines.

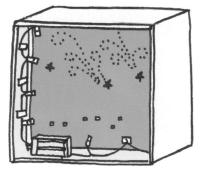

11 Stick this last layer in the frame. Place the lights just inside the frame, spacing them evenly and using masking tape to secure in position. If you like, make a hole in the gray paper (near the bottom) and poke one of the lights through to get more light between the different layers.

12 Place the battery pack in the left-hand corner of the frame, using a dab of glue to stop it from moving around.

13 In the left-hand corner of the gray card stock (card), cut a hole big enough to get your finger through, to turn the light switch on and off. Dab glue all around the back edge of the frame and stick the card stock (card) in place.

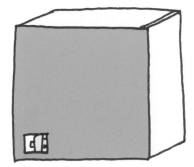

Dazzling peacock

I recently discovered paint in a pen! It's a brilliant craft tool for projects like this, and makes it so much easier to achieve a straight, even line than when using a paintbrush. It means that you can have this beautiful bird up on your wall in no time. The overlaid shapes are cut from tissue paper. It's a simple technique that creates gorgeous tones of color where the papers overlap.

1 Follow the instructions to make the projector. Enlarge the bird and plant templates by 400%. Place the piece of glass from the projector over the templates and draw the design on the glass using a black felt-tip pen. Use masking tape to stick the glass into position over the hole in the projector, reversing the image.

You will need

Posterboard (cardboard) projector (see page 8)

Templates, page 142

Black felt-tip pen

Masking tape

Pencil

A paint pen (or a very thick felt-tip pen)

Plain or graph paper

Scissors

Tissue paper in a mix of colors

Spray adhesive

Face mask

2 In a darkened room, project the image onto the wall, moving the box and light source around until you are happy with the size and position—make sure the peacock's feet are close to the baseboard (skirting board). Use a pencil to draw the outline.

3 Go over the pencil lines using the paint pen or thick felt-tip pen.

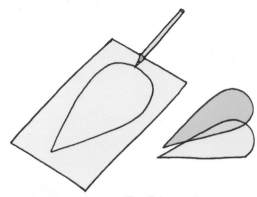

4 Enlarge the templates for the peacock to the right size using a photocopier. Alternatively, scale it up using graph paper. Cut these out.

5 Use a pencil to draw round the templates onto tissue paper and cut out the shapes. Make a few in each size from different colors.

6 Give a light spray of adhesive to the tissue-paper shapes and stick them in position as shown in the photograph on the previous page. Overlap the shapes to create lovely color changes. Always read the manufacturer's instructions when using spray adhesive, and wear a face mask.

Wall flowers

Create these stylish floral decorations from a few sheets of giftwrap. Grouped together in different sizes they make an elegant display. The flowers are backed with foamboard, so they are light enough to mount using sticky tack—ideal if you don't want to use hooks or nails. If you're looking for a decoration for a wedding-photo wall, these would be perfect—get your friends to help you make them.

You will need

Something circular to draw around

Pencil

Foamboard

Craft knife

Cutting mat

Template, page 138

Tracing paper

Masking tape

Paper

Scissors

Sheets of patterned paper or thin card stock (card)

Craft glue

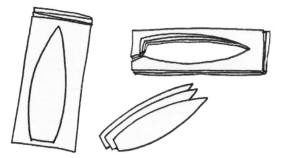

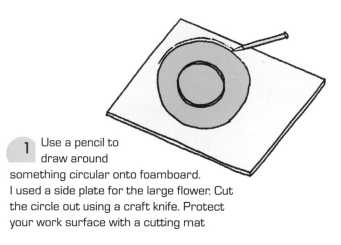

1 Use a pencil to draw around something circular onto foamboard. I used a side plate for the large flower. Cut the circle out using a craft knife. Protect your work surface with a cutting mat

2 Enlarge and trace out the petal shape, then cut it out to make a template. A quick way to make multiple petals is to cut a long strip of paper with a width that matches the length of the template. Concertina-fold the strip of paper a few times, place the template on top, and cut around it using scissors.

3 Fold each petal in half lengthways and then open out again, so that each one has a crease down the center.

4 Dab some glue at the stem end of each petal and stick to the foamboard circle, placing the ends 1 in. (3 cm) into the circle and so that the crease is facing up. Stick petals all around the edge of the circle, keeping them close together.

5 Stick down a second row of petals with the bases 2¾ in. (7 cm) into the circle so that you cover the bases of the first row of petals.

6 Continue with a third row of petals, placing the bases 4½ in. (11 cm) into the circle.

7 Stick a final circle of petals at the center so that all the foamboard is covered.

8 Cut a small circle of paper to stick at the center of the flower.

big
and bold

Gallery wall

It is impossible to flick through an interiors magazine without spotting a few gallery walls. Why not make your own? All you need are a handful of paper-cutting and painting techniques and a roll of washi tape! I used aluminum frames to mount my artworks, but there are no rules here. Mix and match your frames if you prefer. Similarly, you can follow the instructions to complete the look I have created or adapt them to make a wall of pictures that is all you!

1 Cut one piece of cartridge paper to the same size as each frame, and then cut a few extra. Use a ruler and pencil to mark the measurements and a craft knife for the cutting. Protect your work surface with a cutting mat.

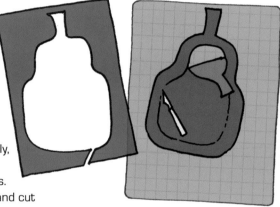

2 To make the pear, I used a frame measuring 27½ x 20 in. (70 x 50 cm). Enlarge the template for the outline of the pear to the right size using a photocopier. Alternatively, scale it up using graph paper. It is quite big, so you will have to use two ledger-size (A3) sections. Trace out the shape, transfer it to black paper, and cut out the outline.

You will need

Frames in different sizes

Thick white cartridge paper

Ruler

Pencil

Craft knife

Cutting mat

Templates, pages 140 and 141

Ledger-size (A3) plain or graph paper

Tracing paper

Masking tape

Large sheet of black paper

Letter-size (A4) sheets of thin paper in blue and green

Small, sharp scissors

Craft (PVA) glue

Black paint

Paintbrushes

Washi tape

Foamboard

Tissue paper in various colors

Spray adhesive

Face mask

Eraser

Hammer

Nails

3 Fold a sheet of blue paper in half, horizontally. Enlarge and trace the template for the smaller leaf and position it, face down, on the folded paper. The straight edge of the trace should align with the fold. Go over the pencil lines to transfer the design to the paper.

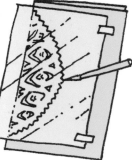

4 Use sharp scissors to cut out the leaf shape and all the little triangles around the edge. You can then cut the pattern into the leaf by folding it, one section at a time, as marked on the template. Open it up and smooth it out gently.

5 Repeat Steps 3 and 4— using green paper—to make the larger leaf. Make the stalk section in the same way.

6 Position all four sections of the pear design on white cartridge paper and glue in position.

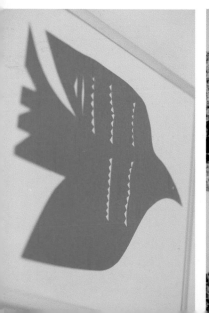

7 For the paper-cut bird I used a frame measuring 12 x 8¼ in. (30 x 21 cm). Trace out the template and transfer it to a sheet of thin blue paper. Use a craft knife on a cutting mat to cut out the shape. Use craft (PVA) glue to stick the bird on a piece of cartridge paper.

8 To make the abstract, black-and-white, paper-cut design, I used a 20 x 16 in. (50 x 40 cm) frame. You can follow the template for this piece, but I think it's also good to experiment and create something individual. Start by making some bold brushstrokes in black paint on a sheet of cartridge paper. Experiment with different textures. Paint some circles, too, making sure you can still see some brushstrokes.

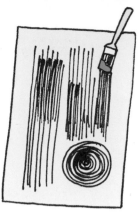

9 When the paint is dry, cut out some shapes and experiment with different arrangements. Include some of the offcuts, too, as they can help to make a bold positive/negative, light/dark design. When you are happy with your arrangement, stick it down using craft (PVA) glue. For contrast, I have added a section of green paper, cut from the cover of a catalog.

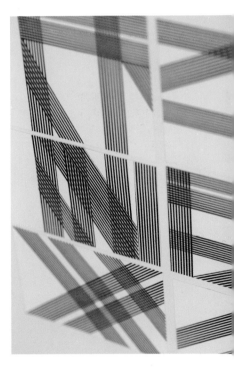

10 The black-and-white looped artwork is an offcut from my experiments with the piece made in Steps 8 and 9. The frame measures 12 x 8¼ in. (30 x 21 cm).

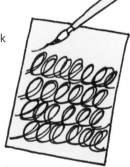

11 The black-and-white grid-like artwork is in a frame measuring 16 x 12 in. (40 x 30 cm). Using washi tape, make up a ledger-size (A3) sheet of lines, triangles, and geometric shapes. Cut rectangular sections from this and group them together on a sheet of cartridge paper. When you are happy with the arrangement, glue the shapes in place.

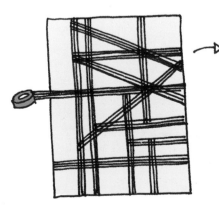

12 To make the large letter "d," simply print off a large letter from the computer. Glue this to some foamboard and cut it out using a craft knife on a cutting mat.

13 The brightly colored triangle artwork is in a frame measuring 16 x 12 in. (40 x 30 cm). Draw a pencil line 1 in. (3 cm) in from the left-hand edge of the paper. Cut four triangles from colored tissue paper, each measuring 4¾ in. (12 cm) along the base and 10 in. (25 cm) in height. Stick these overlapping each other and aligning their bases with the pencil line. Use spray adhesive and follow the manufacturer's instructions—you should wear a mask. Erase the pencil line.

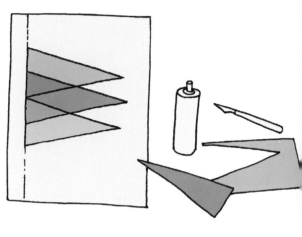

14 The little black-and-white bird is taken from the template for the project on the opposite page.

15 Once you have framed all of your artworks, place them on the floor in different positions until you are happy with the arrangement. Take a photograph of the arrangement so that you can refer to it as you start placing the pictures on the wall. Hammer a nail into the wall to hang each frame.

16 If you feel you need more works of art, you can always add to your gallery. I added some picture-postcard-sized offcuts and a wire letter that I felt fitted the scheme.

Beautiful bird

I have painted this striking design straight onto the wall, which I think gives it more wow factor. You could paint it onto a board or canvas, if you prefer. You can change the look of your bird through your choice of colors—bright and zingy or pretty and pale. The technique involves painting one color over the top of another. Bear this in mind, as it does change the color of the top coat a little.

You will need

Posterboard (cardboard) projector (see page 8)

Template, page 139

Black felt-tip pen

Masking tape

Pencil

Paint in two colors

Paintbrushes

1 Follow the instructions to make the projector. Enlarge the bird template by 200%. Place the piece of glass from the projector over the template and draw the bird design on the glass using a black felt-tip pen.

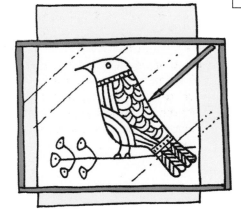

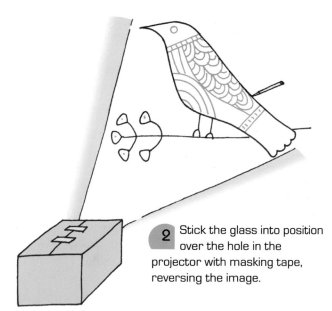

2 Stick the glass into position over the hole in the projector with masking tape, reversing the image.

3 In a darkened room, project the image onto the wall, moving the box around until you are happy with the size and position. Use a pencil to draw just the outline of the bird and the branch.

4 Paint the whole of the bird shape and branch in the color you have chosen for the base design. Allow the paint to dry.

5 Return the projector to the same position and use pencil to draw in the top design that goes over the bird.

6 Using the color you have chosen for the top design, carefully paint over all the lines you drew in Step 5, using a small paintbrush. The lines need to be ½ in. (1.5 cm) wide and should overlap the outside edge of the bird—on top of the base design. Your lines should completely cover the legs and main part of the branch.

7 Give the shapes at the end of the branch an outline in the same way and finish each shape with a dot at the center.

Leaping hare

Use washi tape in a zingy color to create this fun, geometric artwork. Make it big and bold for a feature on a large wall. Washi tape comes in every color and pattern imaginable, so you may want to make your design spotty, floral, stripy, neon, or a combination of these. If you haven't used washi tape before, be warned: once you start looking at the many colors and styles available, you may become addicted!

You will need

Posterboard (cardboard) projector (see page 8)

Template, page 141

Black felt-tip pen

Masking tape

Pencil

Washi tape

Scissors

Craft knife

Eraser

1 Follow the instructions to make the projector.

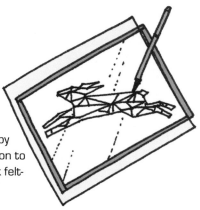

2 Enlarge the hare template by 200%. Trace the template on to the projector glass, using a black felt-tip pen.

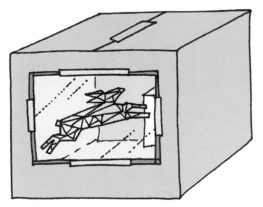

3 Place the glass over the hole in the projector and stick in place using masking tape. Make sure the image is in reverse.

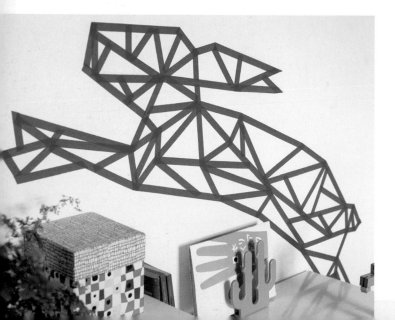

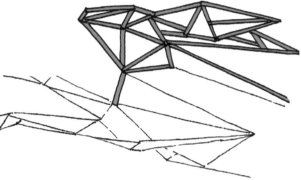

4 In a darkened room, project the image onto the wall, moving the box around until you are happy with the size and position.

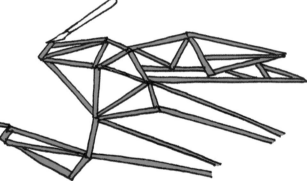

5 Trace over the projected lines using a pencil, then cut strips of washi tape and place them along all the pencil lines.

6 Try to keep the edges and corners of your design sharp. If you have any overlapping washi tape, use a craft knife to cut it away.

7 Erase any pencil lines that still show.

Little blackboard town

This project is easy to create, looks stylish, and provides entertainment for the kids. What's not to love? Blackboard paint is easily obtainable at DIY stores and even comes in different colors. I have used traditional black for contrast with the bright patterns. The roofs and the trees are made from sheets of giftwrap and a wallpaper offcut, so all very affordable.

You will need

Newspaper

Scissors

Masking tape in different widths

Pencil

Blackboard paint

Paintbrush

Patterned paper

Long ruler

Craft (PVA) glue

Craft knife

Cutting mat

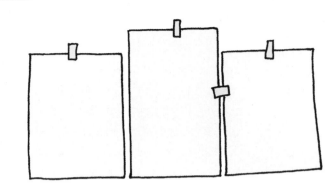

1 Decide how big you want your houses to be. Cut or fold to size, one sheet of newspaper for each house and position it on the wall using masking tape. The houses don't have to be the same size—a little variation is good. Leave small gaps between them—mine were ½ in. (1 cm) wide.

2 Draw around the newspaper using a pencil, then remove the newspaper. Mask off each house with masking tape, using your pencil lines as guides. I used thin masking tape between the houses and thicker tape around the edges.

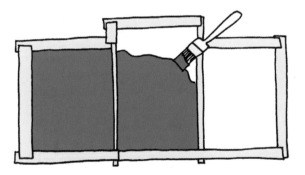

3 Paint the house shapes with the blackboard paint and leave the paint to dry before carefully peeling off the masking tape.

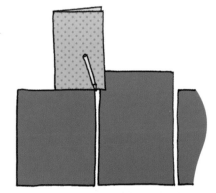

4 Mark the center of the each house shape, along the top edge. Fold a piece of patterned paper in half and align the fold, vertically, with the center mark of one of the houses. Mark the edge of the house (as shown) on the patterned paper.

5 Use a ruler to draw a line from the mark you have just made on the patterned paper diagonally, up to the folded edge. Cut along this line using scissors.

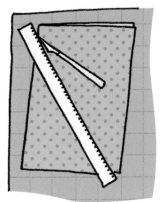

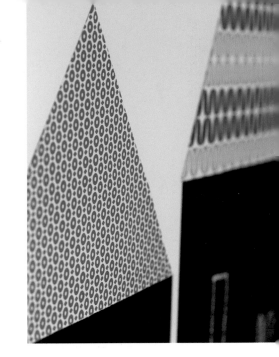

6 Open up the triangle you have made and glue it to the wall, aligning the straight edge with the top of the house.

7 Repeat Steps 4 to 6 to make two more roofs. You can make them different heights.

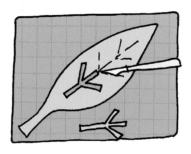

8 Draw a simple tree shape on the back of the paper you have chosen for a tree. I have made a simple pointed oval. Cut this out. Draw in a few branches and cut these out using a craft knife and protecting your work surface with a cutting mat. Stick the tree on the wall next to the houses.

Silver spot bike

Turn a dull hallway into an exciting part of the house with this big-idea project. You may have an expanse of wall that is crying out for something, and this stylishly graphic bicycle couldn't be easier to achieve. My bike is a shimmering silver, but these large stickers come in all colors—how about neon yellow for an art piece that really pops?!

You will need

Posterboard (cardboard) projector (see page 8)

Template, page 139

Black felt-tip pen

Masking tape

Pencil

Long ruler

String

Mapping or drawing pin

Large adhesive dots

Eraser

1 Follow the instructions to make the projector. Enlarge the bicycle template by 200%. Place the piece of glass from the projector over the template and draw the design on to the glass using a black felt-tip pen

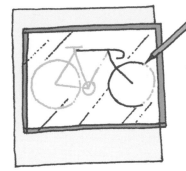

2 Stick the glass into position over the hole in the projector using masking tape, reversing the image. Project the design onto the wall, moving the box around until you have the size you want and the base of the wheels are close to the floor.

3 Draw out the design in pencil. Draw in the dot that marks the center of each wheel. You can start positioning the dots at this stage, but I think it is better to first sharpen up the lines, using a ruler for the straight lines.

4 To sharpen up the wheel lines, use masking tape to attach a length of string to the pencil, close to the lead end.

5 Position the pencil lead on the wheel outline you have already drawn from the projector. Pull the string taut and pin the loose end to the wall at the wheel's center point. Redraw the outline, keeping the string taut all the time.

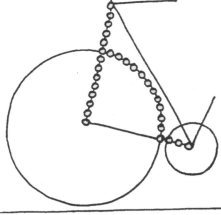

6 Fill in the outline using adhesive dots. I left a small space between each dot. Visually, aim to get the pencil line directly beneath the middle of each dot.

7 You may need to adjust the spacing a little when completing the wheels, or where lines cross, in order to keep the line continuous. In such instances, it is useful to place a dot gently to start with, so you can easily reposition it if need be.

8 Erase any visible pencil lines.

Box-frame wall

Don't be put off by this project because it involves woodwork. The frames are very easy to make and, once you have assembled the piece and styled it beautifully, you won't be disappointed! I have painted my frames in pretty pastel colors to show off a selection of vintage floral ephemera, little cups, old picture postcards, and paper scraps. You can choose to use any colors you like.

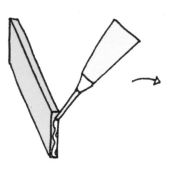

1 To make a frame, take one length of wood of each size. Spread wood glue on one end of the shorter length of wood, as shown, and align it with the face of the longer length, at one end.

You will need

Wood (see Tip)

Wood glue

Panel pins

Hammer

Paint

Paintbrush

Nails for hanging

Tip: Frame sizes

I made my frames in two sizes using wood measuring 2¾ in. (6.8 cm) wide by ½ in. (1 cm) thick:
Large: 13 x 10 in. (33 x 25.5 cm)
Small: 10 x 8 in. (25.5 x 20 cm)
You can cut the wood from long lengths or get them cut to the right length at your local hardware store.

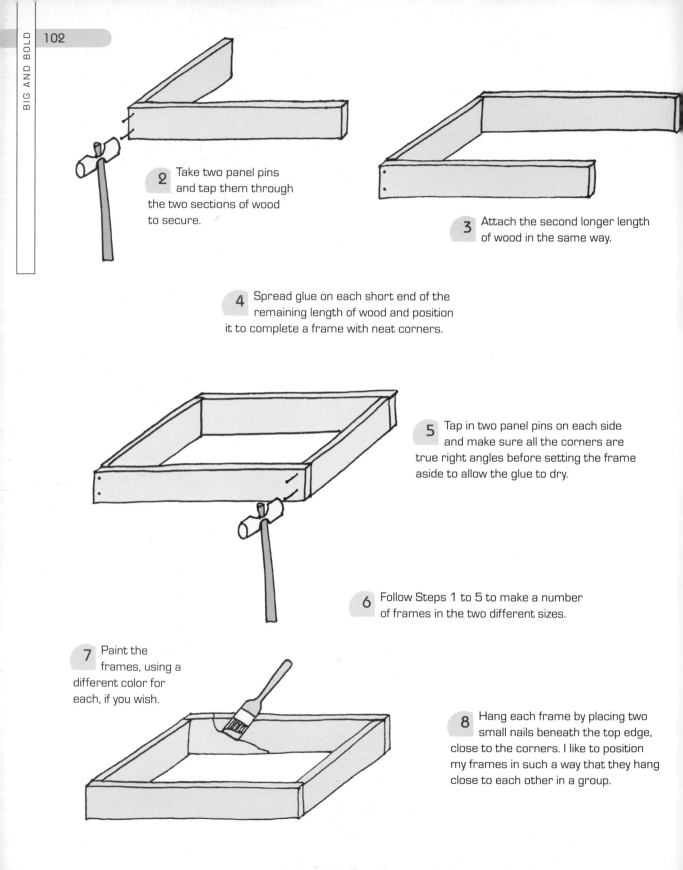

2 Take two panel pins and tap them through the two sections of wood to secure.

3 Attach the second longer length of wood in the same way.

4 Spread glue on each short end of the remaining length of wood and position it to complete a frame with neat corners.

5 Tap in two panel pins on each side and make sure all the corners are true right angles before setting the frame aside to allow the glue to dry.

6 Follow Steps 1 to 5 to make a number of frames in the two different sizes.

7 Paint the frames, using a different color for each, if you wish.

8 Hang each frame by placing two small nails beneath the top edge, close to the corners. I like to position my frames in such a way that they hang close to each other in a group.

Swinging monkeys

Bring the jungle into your home with a group of cheeky monkeys swinging across the wall. Cut from sheets of brightly patterned giftwrap or offcuts of wallpaper, these critters are quick to make and guaranteed to add a sense of fun and adventure to a kid's bedroom. Stick the first monkey so that it looks as if it is swinging from a shelf or a hook on the wall. Then add more monkeys in different sizes. Use their curly tails, hands, or feet to hang them in different arrangements.

You will need

Templates, page 142

Plain or graph paper

Pencil

Masking tape

Scissors

Patterned paper

Tracing paper

Colored paper

Craft (PVA) glue

1 Enlarge the monkey templates to the right sizes on a photocopier. You will need to do this in sections and stick the photocopies together. Alternatively, scale the monkeys up using graph paper. Cut out the monkeys to use as templates.

2 Lay a sheet of patterned paper face down on your work surface and place the template for the larger monkey on top. Secure with a few pieces of masking tape, draw around the shape using pencil, and cut it out. Turn the template over to make a monkey facing the opposite direction—they can face either way.

3 Trace out the heart and face shapes. Transfer these to colored or patterned paper and cut them out.

4 Spread the backs of the heart and face with glue and stick them in position on the monkey.

5 Trace out the shapes for the eyes, nose, and mouth. Transfer these onto colored paper, cut them out, and stick them in position on the monkey.

6 Repeat Steps 1 to 5 to make a number of smaller monkeys. Stick them to the wall, overlapping hands over tails in any combination you like.

Neon pop art

A book on wall art would not be complete without a graffiti-type project. I have worked with stencils before, but not to this scale and not using spray paint, so this was a new challenge for me. I opted for the brightest possible color—a neon pink and I am so glad I did, as the color really pops. You can create this effect using any photo; the children, your partner, or even the family pet! You need to be able to work on the photograph on a computer and get the picture photocopied to ANSI D (A1) size, but the effort is well worth it. Be brave, go big and bold, and make a statement!

You will need

Photograph

Computer

Craft knife

Cutting mat

Newspaper

Spray adhesive

Face mask

Masking tape

Spray paint

1 Find a suitable photograph and upload it to the computer. Choose an image that is high in contrast, as this will create more dramatic shadows. Make the image black-and-white and then play around with the effects and contrast until you are happy with the look. Print the image out and have it enlarged to ANSI D (A1) size.

2 Using a craft knife, and protecting your work surface with a cutting mat, cut away the black areas in the image. If, like mine, your picture has areas that go right up to the edge of the paper, don't cut to the edge, but leave a ¾ in. (2 cm) border.

3 Try to keep the cuts simple. You can be selective on such areas as the hair, cutting away large sections and leaving just a few small highlights. The image should look very graphic with blocks of color. If you remove pieces by mistake, keep them to one side as you can still use them.

4 Turn the stencil over and lay it on some newspaper. Spray it very lightly with adhesive. Always read the manufacturer's instructions when using spray adhesive, and wear a face mask.

5 Now position the stencil on the wall. It will be quite flimsy, so you may need to get help with this. Flatten the stencil down and stick on any small pieces that you cut off by mistake. Mask the edges of the stencil and protect the wall around the stencil with newspaper—stick it down using masking tape.

6 Read the instructions for using the spray paint and spray the image through the stencil. Make sure you wear a face mask.

7 When you have finished spraying, carefully remove the newspaper and masking tape. Peel off the stencil to reveal your image.

Floral dress

I have made this pretty, 1950s-inspired dress using the decorative art of découpage. I painted the dress straight onto the wall and then embellished it with a collection of cut-out floral scraps. It is so simple to do and the results are stunning. You can use any paper—old giftwrap, craft paper, or wallpaper samples. I also added some leaves and branches cut from the pages of a book that I rescued from the recycling. I love the contrast of the black-and-white with the bright colours—it adds perfectly to that vintage appeal.

You will need

Posterboard (cardboard) projector (see page 8)

Templates, page 140

Black felt-tip pen

Masking tape

Pencil

Paint

Paintbrush

Scraps of floral paper

Pages from an old book or magazine

Scissors

Craft (PVA) glue

Tracing paper

1 Follow the instructions for making the projector. Enlarge the template by 200%. Place the piece of glass from the projector over the template and draw the dress and coat hanger on the glass using a black felt-tip pen. Use masking tape to stick the glass into position over the hole in the projector.

2 In a darkened room, project the image onto the wall, moving the box and light source around until you are happy with the size and position. Use a pencil to draw just the outline of the dress and the coat hanger.

3 Paint the dress in a color of your choice.

4 When the paint is dry, use the projector again to draw in the lines for the branches.

5 Cut some flowers and leaves from your papers. I also cut out some butterflies. Cut strips of paper from an old book or magazine for the branches. I made mine ¼ in. (5 mm) wide. Cut out some leaf shapes from an old book.

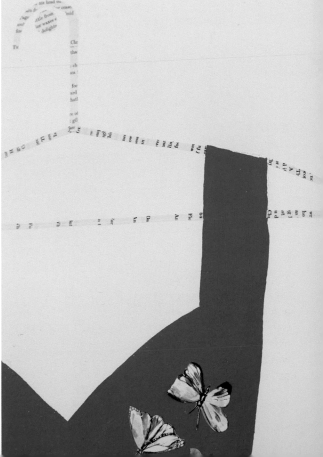

6 Stick the branches down first, using craft (PVA) glue. Follow your pencil lines as a guide.

7 Now stick the flowers, leaves, and butterflies onto the dress. I stuck quite a few along the base of the dress and then along the branches, interspersed with some of the leaves cut from the book pages.

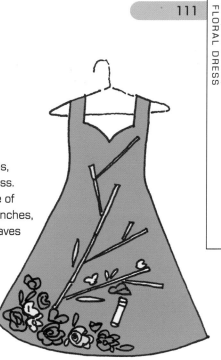

8 Trace over the coat hanger section and transfer the shape onto a page from a book. Cut it out, making the width ¼ in. (5 mm).

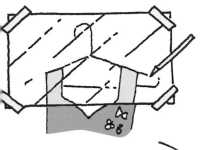

9 Position the coat hanger on the wall and glue in place. Finish with a small "hook" cut from a book page, from which the coat hanger can hang.

shapes
and colors

Magnetic puzzle board

Shopping in a hardware store recently, I was amazed by the sheer variety of specialist paints available now—paints for every surface and with a multitude of different finishes. The one that caught my eye was the magnetic paint. So I decided to create a puzzle board on the wall, complete with tangram shapes, for an ever-changing picture. A tangram is an ancient puzzle invented in China. It consists of eight shapes that are cut from a square in such a way that they can make thousands of different arrangements.

You will need

Pencil

Ruler

Triangle (set square)

Masking tape

Magnetic paint

Second color paint

Paintbrushes

Craft (PVA) glue

Colored paper

Foamboard

Craft knife

Cutting mat

Template, page 140

Tracing paper

Self-adhesive magnetic strip

Scissors

1 Mark out a square on the wall using a pencil, ruler, and triangle (set square). I made mine 24 x 24 in. (60 x 60 cm).

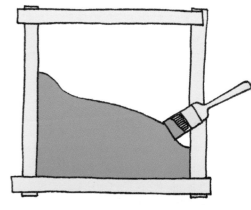

2 Mask off the edges of the lines you have drawn with masking tape and paint a layer of metallic paint in the square within. Wait for this to dry before applying a second coat.

3 When this is dry, paint over the metallic paint in a second color. When all the paint is dry, carefully remove the masking tape.

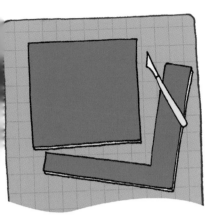

4 Use craft (PVA) glue to stick a sheet of colored paper to some foamboard and cut out a square measuring 6¼ x 6¼ in. (16 x 16 cm). Use a craft knife, and protect your work surface with a cutting mat.

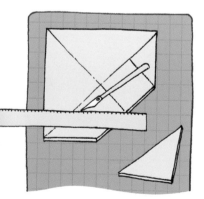

5 Enlarge the template for the tangram to the right size on a photocopier and cut it out. Alternatively, scale it up using graph paper. Trace out the template and transfer it to the back of the foamboard. Cut out the shapes.

6 Attach strips of self-adhesive magnetic strip to the back of each shape, place them on the wall, and play!

Copper blocks

Small works of art grouped together can make a delightful display of abstract color. Here, the gorgeous copper leaf shimmers in the changing light, making an eye-catching feature. This is a great project for doing your own thing. I have used wooden blocks for this project, but small, ready-made canvases would work well too. I have drawn up seven different templates to get you started on shapes and layout. Experiment with different arrangements and when you are happy get sticking!

You will need

Wooden blocks in various sizes. Mine were cut from 3¼ x 1½ in. (8.5 x 3.5 cm) planks. I cut lengths measuring 5½ in. (14 cm), 4 in. (10 cm), and 3¼ in. (8.5cm)

White paint

Paintbrush

Templates, page 140

Colored paper

Craft knife

Cutting mat

Ruler

Craft (PVA) glue

Copper leaf (the rub-down type with backing paper)

Tracing paper

Pencil

Scissors

Spray adhesive

Face mask

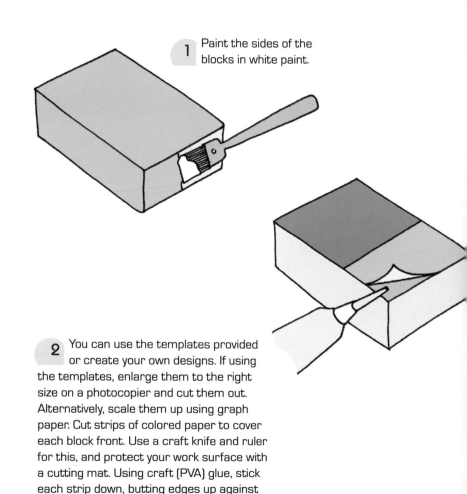

1 Paint the sides of the blocks in white paint.

2 You can use the templates provided or create your own designs. If using the templates, enlarge them to the right size on a photocopier and cut them out. Alternatively, scale them up using graph paper. Cut strips of colored paper to cover each block front. Use a craft knife and ruler for this, and protect your work surface with a cutting mat. Using craft (PVA) glue, stick each strip down, butting edges up against each other for a nice, flat surface.

3 Use the templates to make shapes from the copper leaf. Enlarge the templates to the right size and use a pencil to draw each shape onto tracing paper and transfer it to the reverse (backing paper side) of the copper leaf. Cut different shapes, if you like, and make circles of different sizes. Use scissors to cut curved edges.

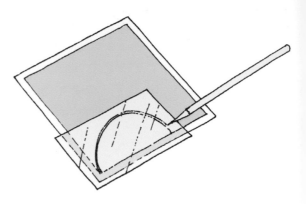

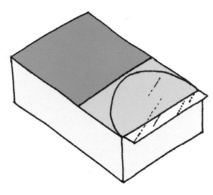

4 Coat the surface of the copper leaf pieces with a thin layer of spray adhesive. Always follow the manufacturer's instructions when using this glue—you should wear a mask. Carefully pick up each shape by the overlapping edge of the backing paper (see Tip) and lay it, copper side down, in position on the block.

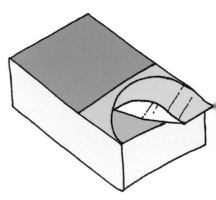

5 Peel off the backing paper. Lay a piece of tracing paper over the top of the shape and rub down smoothly.

Tip: Copper leaf

When cutting the copper leaf, draw each shape so that one edge is right on the outer edge of the copper leaf. This will give you a small overlapping section of backing paper to hold when sticking down the copper leaf.

Marquee arrow

Light up a section of wall and give your room an urban-cool vibe with this industrial-look, illuminated arrow. The string of LED lights is battery operated, so there are no unsightly wires to deal with.

You will need

Template, page 142

Ledger-size (A3) plain paper or graph paper

Pencil

Ruler

Scissors

Thick card stock (card) in two different colors

Masking tape

Craft knife

Cutting mat

Craft (PVA) glue

Awl (bradawl), or similar, for making smaller holes

Knitting needle, or similar, for making larger holes

String of 20 LED battery-operated lights

2 small blocks of wood, each measuring 1½ x 1½ x 1 in. (4 x 4 x 2.5 cm)

1 Enlarge the template to the right size using a photocopier and cut it out. You will need to work in two sections on ledger-size (A3) sheets of paper and join them together. Alternatively, scale up using graph paper to make a template for each size arrow.

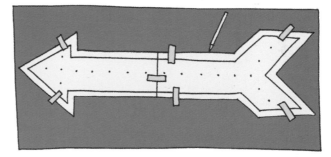

2 If you are using the photocopy method, cut out the template and lay it down on colored card stock (card) for the border section. Secure with masking tape and draw around the edge using pencil. Cut this out, using the craft knife and protecting your work surface with a cutting mat.

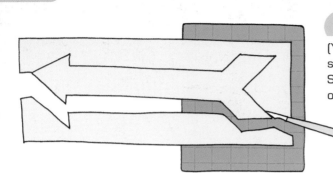

3 Trim the border section from the template so that you are left with the smaller arrow. (You will not need to do this if you scaled up two separate templates using graph paper.) Follow Step 2 to cut an arrow from a contrasting color of card stock (card).

4 Use craft glue (PVA) to stick the smaller arrow on top of the larger arrow, leaving an even border all around.

5 Mark positions for the lights. If using the photocopy method, center the small arrow template over the back of your arrow shape, and press the awl (bradawl) through at each dot. Remove the template and pierce each hole a second time, using a knitting needle to make the holes bigger. The lightbulbs should fit snugly into the holes.

6 Push each bulb into a hole from the back. I used 19 of the 20 bulbs, as that worked best with my measurements. Tape the battery pack to the back of the arrow.

7 Stick the two blocks of wood to the back of the arrow—one at either end. You can use these to rest on nails, for hanging.

Stylish stencil

It is a bold move to paint a design straight onto the wall. But this can make a stunning focal point in an otherwise plain section of a room. Choosing the right colors is important. I based mine on some of my favorite vintage pots and bowls. A good way to get a mix of colors that you are happy with is by cutting up bits of colored paper and laying them down next to each other in different combinations.

You will need

Templates, page 143

Plain or graph paper

Tracing paper

Masking tape

Pencil

Stencil card stock (card)

Craft knife

Cutting mat

Tape measure

Paint in three colors

Stencil brush

Eraser

1 Enlarge the templates to the right size using a photocopier. Alternatively, scale them up using graph paper. Trace them out and transfer them to stencil card stock (card). Cut them out using a craft knife and protecting your work surface with a cutting mat.

2 The complete design measures 59 x 22½ in. (150 x 57 cm). Mark the baseline on your wall using a tape measure and pencil—you may need to get someone to help you with this.

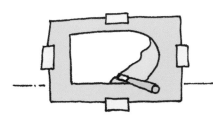

3 Starting on the left-hand side, position the stencil on the baseline and secure with some masking tape.

4 Apply the first coat of paint, using a stencil brush and a gentle stabbing motion.

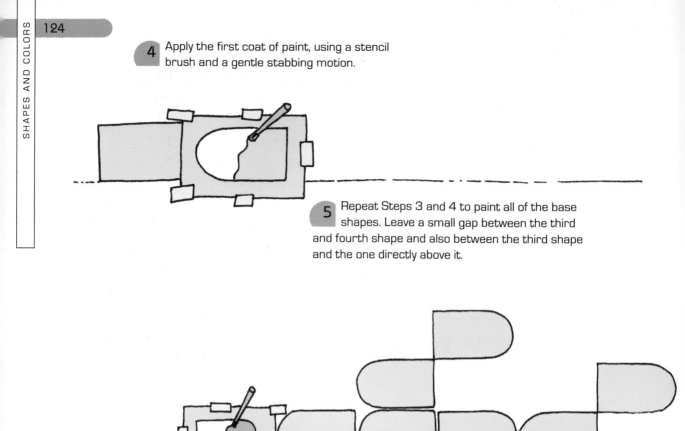

5 Repeat Steps 3 and 4 to paint all of the base shapes. Leave a small gap between the third and fourth shape and also between the third shape and the one directly above it.

6 Allow the paint to dry before painting the second color. Position the stencil so that the bottom edge of the card stock (card) aligns with the bottom edge of the base shape and the straight edge of the cut section lines up with the straight edge of base shape. Paint this section and repeat with all the other shapes.

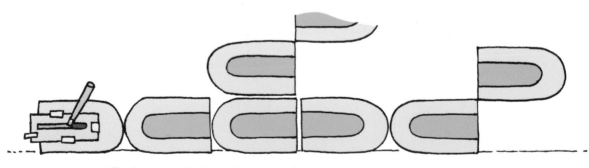

7 Apply the final color in exactly the same way, using the last template. Erase any pencil lines.

Reclaimed wood

I was very lucky to find a stack of old wooden shelves in a flea market recently. I bought four of them. I didn't know what I was going to do with them at the time, but I just knew that I loved the character of the grainy, worn wood and the strip of metal at the top and bottom. I ended up painting on them and soon realized that they make a great base for a piece of artwork. Simple eye-catching shapes work best. I have designed a fish shape to go in my seaside home, but because the fish is stylized and graphic, I think it would look fantastic in any interior, adding that bit of industrial styling that is so current in interior design. If you can't find any salvaged wood suitable to paint on, a length of plywood could work really well, too.

1 Join together two sheets of newspaper with some masking tape. Cut the length down so that it is a little shorter than the length of the wood.

2 Fold the newspaper in half lengthways and draw the shape of half a fish up to the fold line, as shown. Make sure that it will fit within the width of your wooden panel. Cut the fish shape out.

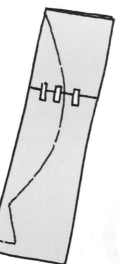

You will need

Newspaper

Masking tape

Length of wood

Scissors

Soft pencil

White paint

Paintbrush

Eraser

Lino-cutting tool or craft knife

Black ink-stamping pad

3 Place the newspaper fish on the panel of wood and secure with some masking tape. Draw around the shape using a soft pencil.

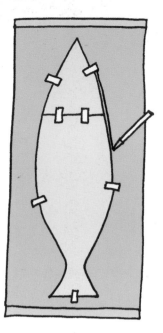

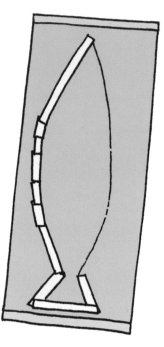

4 Apply masking tape to the outside edge of your pencil line. Use long strips on any straight sections and small strips around the curves.

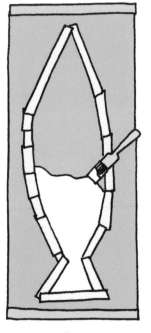

5 Use white paint to fill in the fish shape—you may need to give it two coats for a good coverage.

6 While the paint is drying, make a rubber stamp. I used a large eraser and cut a circle 1 in. (3 cm) across. Then I cut a smaller circle in the middle of the larger one using a lino-cutting tool. If you haven't got a lino-cutting tool, it is possible to use a craft knife.

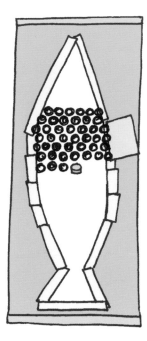

7 Use black ink to print rows of circles on the fish, leaving the head area clear of prints. Take care not to go over the edges of the masking tape and onto the wood. Use scrap paper over the masking tape if you think this might happen.

8 Print one last circle for the eye and leave the ink to dry. Peel away the masking tape.

Shimmer abstract

Simple lines on a large board can create a striking focal point on an empty wall, especially if you use gorgeous, shimmering silver and copper leaf. Try to buy transfer sheets of silver and copper leaf, as this is much easier to handle than loose leaf foils.

1 Paint the wood with white paint and leave to dry. I used matte wall paint.

2 Using a triangle (set square) and ruler, draw a 16½ in. (42 cm) square on the painted wood, positioning it 2 in. (5 cm) from the bottom edge, and centering it between the two side edges, with one corner pointing straight down, as shown.

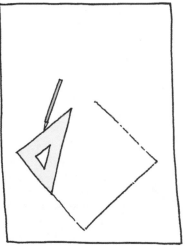

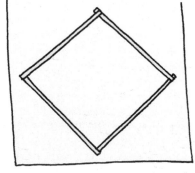

3 Use masking tape to mask all four edges of the shape.

You will need

Wood measuring
40 x 27½ in. (100 x 70 cm)

White paint

Paintbrush

Triangle (set square)

Ruler

Pencil

Masking tape, ½ in.
(1.5 cm) wide

Newspaper

Spray adhesive

Face mask

Copper leaf transfer sheets

Scrap paper

Silver leaf transfer sheets

4 Mask off a second square within the first square, leaving a gap of approximately ½ in. (1.5 mm). I did not want my squares to be exact, so I have positioned the tape by eye. It means some of the gaps between the squares vary slightly in size. Continue to mask off more squares within the squares, until you have a square at the center that measures approximately 2¼ in. (5.5 cm).

5 Mask the board surrounding the largest square with newspaper and secure it with masking tape. Spray the whole area of masked squares lightly with adhesive. Read the instructions for using the adhesive and wear a mask. Remove the newspaper.

6 Cut strips of copper leaf and lay them, one by one, along the glued gaps between the masking tape. Press each strip down well by rubbing over the back of the backing paper and then gently remove the backing paper. Add more copper leaf in areas that have not stuck. It does not matter if the copper overlaps—the joins do not show once it is all rubbed down. Once you have filled all the lines and the square in the middle you can remove the masking tape, gently.

Tip

If you prefer not to use adhesive spray you can use size, the liquid traditionally used for laying down silver and copper leaf. You can buy it in craft stores.

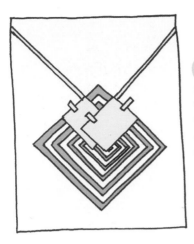

7 Now mask off a 90-degree triangle that extends from the inner corner of the second copper square and out to the side edges of the painted wood, as shown. To avoid placing masking tape on the copper lines (which will lift the copper leaf away on removal), mask this area with some paper, securing the masking tape to the painted wood.

8 Position a second triangle of masking tape 3½ in. (9 cm) away from the first, and a third triangle of masking tape 3½ in. (9 cm) away from the second. Lay some paper over any copper areas and lightly spray the triangles with adhesive.

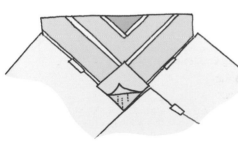

9 Now apply silver leaf in the first two chevron shapes that you made in Step 8 and copper in the triangle shape at the top of the painted wood. Gently remove the masking tape.

10 To finish the piece, add a small silver triangle at the bottom of the painted wood, just below the copper squares. This time, lightly spray adhesive on the silver leaf directly. When cutting the piece of copper leaf, try to leave a section of the backing paper border to hold on to as you lay the leaf in position. Once in position, rub it down and remove the backing paper.

Himmeli wreath

Himmeli straw sculptures are traditionally made in Finland, especially at Christmas time, when they are used for decorating the tree and the house. Not only do they fit in with the love I have for all things Nordic, but also with my passion for all things geometric! Himmeli structures are easy to make and look stunning as wall decorations.

You will need

Paper drinking straws

Scissors

Tape measure

Florist's wire

Wire cutters

1 Cut the straws into 4 in. (10 cm) sections. You need 140 in total. Cut a length of wire measuring 63 in. (160 cm).

2 Thread three straws onto the wire, bending the wire at one end to stop the straws falling off.

3 Arrange the three straws to make a triangle and twist the bent wire from Step 2 around your working section of wire to secure.

4 Thread on two more straws, arranging them to make a second triangle. Poke the twisted end of wire into the first straw. Secure your shape with a twist of the wire at the top corner of the triangle you made in Step 3.

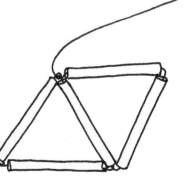

5 Add two more straws, arranging them to make a third triangle. Secure your shape with a knot at the bottom left-hand corner of the triangle you made in Step 3.

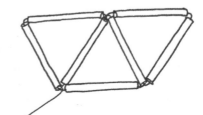

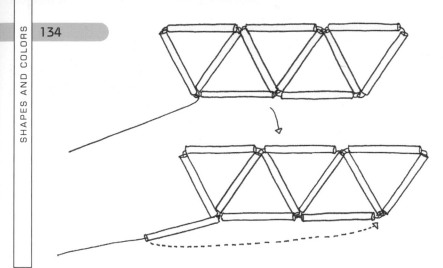

6 Continue to add straws in this way until you have a row of five triangles. With the shape arranged as shown, add one more straw and swing it round to the far-right corner of the shape. This will make a square base, with a triangle on opposite sides, and a pyramid shape below.

7 Secure the base with a twist of the wire, then thread the wire through any one of the straws leading off the base.

8 Bring the two triangles at the sides of the base up to meet each other and secure with a twist of wire at the top. Do not trim the wire.

9 You will now have the basic himmeli diamond shape. Repeat Steps 2 to 8 to make nine more shapes.

10 Take two of the shapes and line them up, point to point, with their wires facing to the right. Push the wire from the left-hand shape into one of the straws on the right-hand shape. Twist the wire around the interconnecting wires to secure. Now trim the wire from the left-hand shape to 1 in. (3 cm), and poke the excess back inside the straw to neaten.

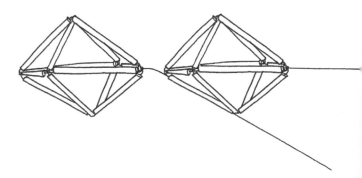

11 Continue to join the shapes together until you have ten in a row. Manipulate the row to make a ring and join the last shape to the first. Trim any excess wire down to 1 in. (3 cm) and push the end of the wire inside one of the straws.

12 Cut a length of wire measuring 47 in. (120 cm). Attach the end of the wire to the inside edge your ring, twisting it around the wires at the bottom point of any one himmeli. Thread on a straw and tuck the short end of the wire inside to neaten.

13 Take the wire along to the bottom point on the next himmeli and wrap the wire around the wires joining the four straws. This makes a joining bar from one shape to the next.

14 Continue to add straws in the same way, until you have come full circle. Wrap the last bit of wire around, trim it to 1 in. (3 cm) and push it into a straw to neaten. This is shown on the diagram with a blue line.

15 Repeat steps 12, 13, and 14 to make connecting bars on the opposite sides of the shapes that you have just completed. This will make another circle of joining bars on the inner section of the joined shapes, which will give strength to the structure. This is shown on the diagram with a pink line.

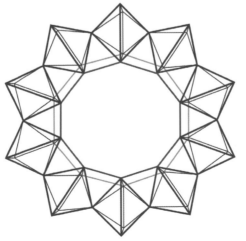

Living wall

Living walls have made a huge impact in the world of interiors during the last few years. Open up the trendiest design magazines and you'll likely find pictures of lush green panels adorning the walls of the most sophisticated and stylish homes. It is not that difficult to make your own living wall and you can pick up everything you need from a DIY store. Vertical indoor greenery raises the humble pot plant to new heights and creates a stunning feature in any contemporary setting. Succulents are ideal for this project.

You will need

2 tongue-and-groove floorboards, each measuring 50 x 8 in. (127 x 20 cm)

Tape measure

Wood saw

Wood glue

Wire mesh measuring 31½ x 20 in. (80 x 50 cm)

Wire cutters

Staple gun

Strip of wood measuring 80 x 1½ in. (200 x 4 cm) and ½ in. (1 cm) in depth

2 plastic seedling trays, the deeper the better

Hammer

Panel pins

Gardening gloves

Plants

Compost

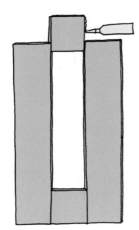

1 To make the frame, use a wood saw to cut a 9½ in. (24 cm) length from one end of each of the floorboards. Run wood glue down each side of the shorter lengths and sandwich them—top and bottom—between the two floorboards, as shown.

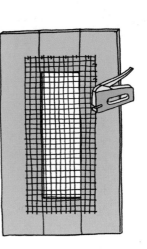

2 Turn the frame over. Place wire mesh over the hole in the frame, with a 4 in. (10 cm) overlap all the way around. Use wire cutters to trim the mesh to the right size and a staple gun to fix it in place.

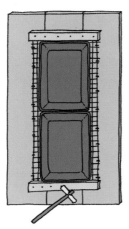

3 Cut two batons from the strip of wood. Make them 4 in. (10 cm) longer than the width of the seedling trays. Arrange the trays over the hole in the frame—face down and short edge to short edge. Keep any overlap with the frame more or less the same top, bottom, and sides. Center the batons above and below the trays, just catching the lips of the trays, and hammer in a couple of panel pins to hold the trays in place. (Hammer in a couple of panel pins from the other side for extra strength, if you like.)

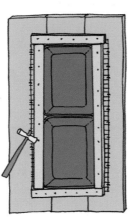

4 Measure the space between top and bottom batons and cut two batons from the strip of wood to the same measurement. Place these batons between the top and bottom batons so that they cover the lips at the side edges of the trays and hammer in panel pins to secure.

5 Turn the frame over. Make cuts in the wire mesh and bend it back on itself so that you can plant the trays. Fill any gaps between the plants with compost and wear gardening gloves to prevent getting scratched by the wire.

6 Water the plants. It is a good idea to leave the frame flat for a few days to let the plants settle and start rooting in. Once mounted, it is best to lift the frame from its position and water the plants while the frame is flat.

Templates

See pages 8–9 for instructions on how to enlarge templates

Beautiful beastie
shown at 25%
page 36

Furry friends trophy heads
shown at 25%
page 46

x4

x2

Inner edge

Guideline for drawing legs

Wall flowers
shown at 50%
page 79

Cactus-pot prints
shown at 50%
page 32

Retro chair
shown at 25%
page 26

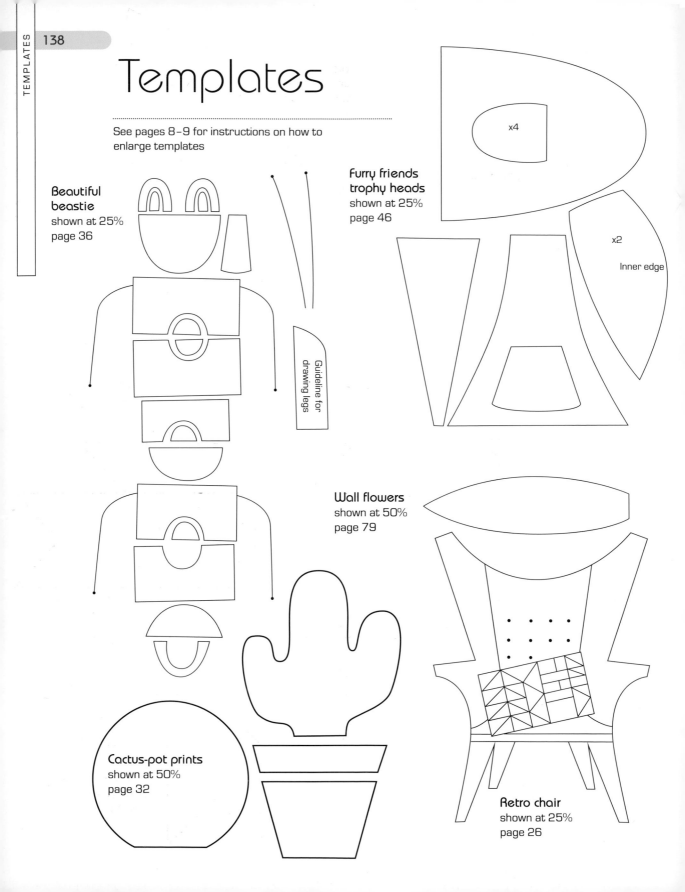

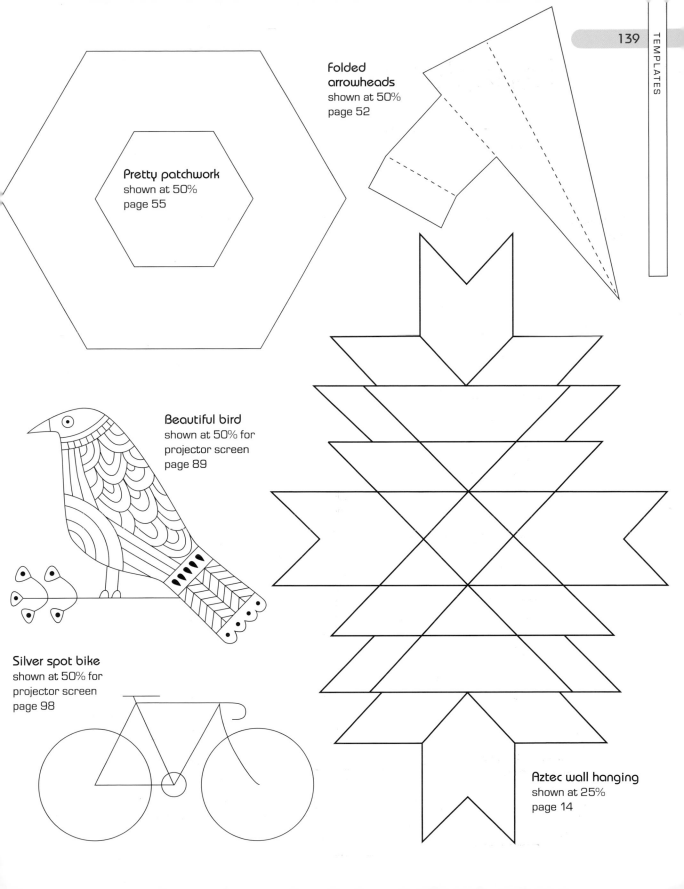

Pretty patchwork
shown at 50%
page 55

Folded arrowheads
shown at 50%
page 52

Beautiful bird
shown at 50% for
projector screen
page 89

Silver spot bike
shown at 50% for
projector screen
page 98

Aztec wall hanging
shown at 25%
page 14

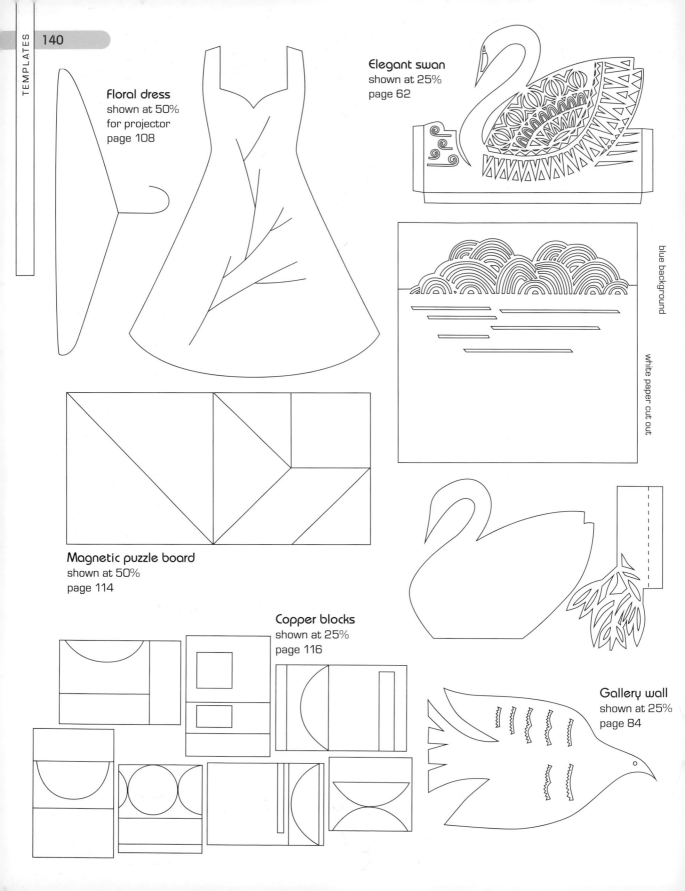

Floral dress
shown at 50%
for projector
page 108

Elegant swan
shown at 25%
page 62

blue background

white paper cut out

Magnetic puzzle board
shown at 50%
page 114

Copper blocks
shown at 25%
page 116

Gallery wall
shown at 25%
page 84

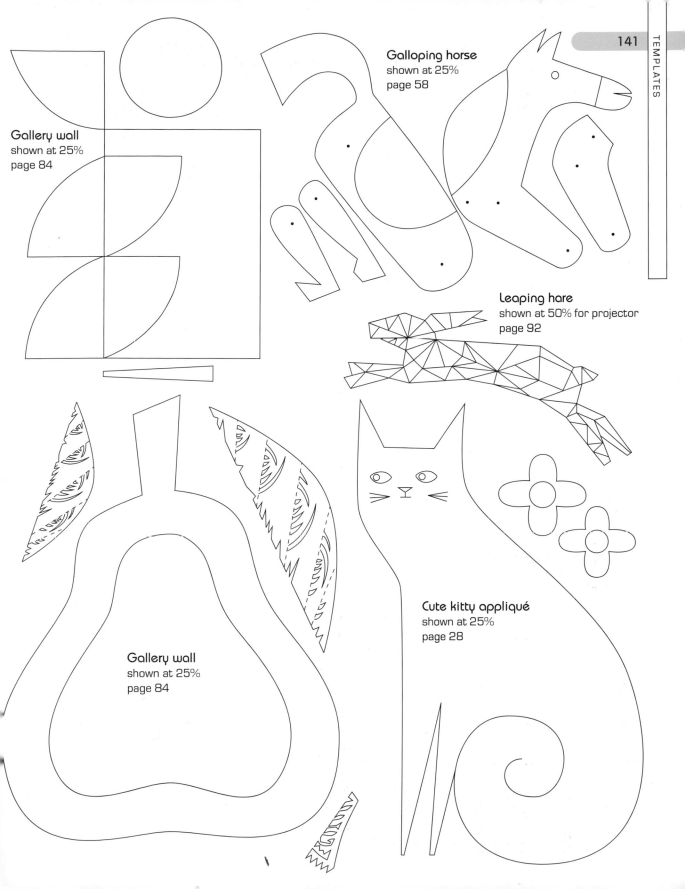

Galloping horse
shown at 25%
page 58

Gallery wall
shown at 25%
page 84

Leaping hare
shown at 50% for projector
page 92

Gallery wall
shown at 25%
page 84

Cute kitty appliqué
shown at 25%
page 28

Dazzling peacock
shown at 50%
page 76

Dazzling peacock
shown at 25% for projector
page 76

Marquee arrow
shown at 12.5%
page 119

Swinging monkies
shown at 25%, for the smaller
monkey, enlarge by 400% and
for the larger monkey, enlarge
by 600%
page XX

x2

Shimmering firefly
shown at 50%
page 66

Shimmering firefly
shown at 12.5%
page 66

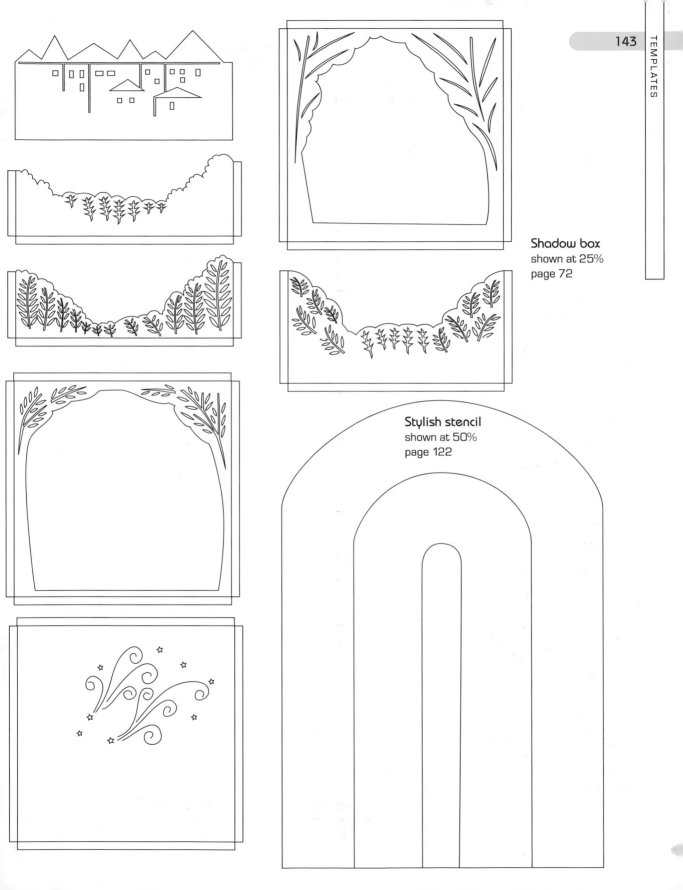

Shadow box
shown at 25%
page 72

Stylish stencil
shown at 50%
page 122

Suppliers

US STOCKISTS

A.C. Moore Stores nationwide
1-888-226-6673
www.acmoore.com
Crafts, etc.
1-800-888-0321
www.craftsetc.com
Craft Site Directory
www.craftsdirectory.com
EvaenAnne
EvaenAnne
http://www.etsy.com/shop/
EvaenAnne
Hobby Lobby
www.hobbylobby.com
Jo-Ann Fabric and Craft Store
1-888-739-4120
www.joann.com
Michaels
1-800-642-4235
www.michaels.com

UK STOCKISTS

Cass Art
020 7354 2999
www.cassart.co.uk
Cloth House
020 7437 5155
www.clothhouse.com
Craft Creations
01992 781900
www.craftcreations.com
Crafty Devils
01271 326777
www.craftydevilspapercraft.co.uk
Homebase
www.homebase.co.uk
Shepherds Papers
020 7233 9999
store.falkiners.com
Hobbycraft
01202 596100
www.hobbycraft.co.uk
Paperchase
www.paperchase.co.uk
The Papercraft Company
07812 575510
www.thepapercraftcompany.co.uk

Index

Acknowledgments

Thank you to CICO Books for giving me the opportunity to work on this lovely project. Working with Cindy, Sally, Anna, and Fahema is always a pleasure. Thanks to the super talented Joanna Henderson for her beautiful photography. Thank you to Anna Southgate. Such careful editing, as always. Thank you to the designer Elizabeth Healey for giving the book such a stylish look. Thanks to Shelly and Sean at etcetera-online.co.uk for letting us shoot in their gorgeous home and letting us use their wonderful props. Thanks as always to my ever supportive family, Milly, Florence, Henrietta, Harvey, and especially my clever and patient husband Ian, who not only gave me the key to his tool shed but joined me in there to help with a couple of projects!

When you smile, your bright eyes twinkle

and your nose begins to crinkle.

Your laughter sets my heart aflutter.

Your warm hugs make
me melt like butter.

I love you when you're in a muddle.

Your tears tell me you
need a cuddle.

Your kisses set
me all aglow.

You have the sweetest face I know.

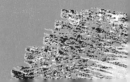

I can't imagine life
without you...

Oh, I love everything about you.

A TEMPLAR BOOK

First published in the UK in 2013 by Templar Publishing
This softback edition published in 2014 by Templar Publishing,
an imprint of The Templar Company Limited,
Deepdene Lodge, Deepdene Avenue, Dorking, Surrey, RH5 4AT
www.templarco.co.uk

Copyright © 2013 by Emma Dodd

1 3 5 7 9 10 8 6 4 2

ISBN: 978-1-84877-175-8

Printed in China